MASTERING

the

NEGOTIATION

PROCESS

A Practical Guide for

the Healthcare Executive

MASTERING

the

NEGOTIATION

PROCESS

A Practical Guide for
the Healthcare Executive

Christopher L. Laubach

Health Administration Press
ACHE Management Series

Your board, staff, or clients may also benefit from this book's insight. For more information on quantity discounts, contact the Health Administration Press Marketing Manager at (312) 424-9470.

This publication is intended to provide accurate and authoritative information in regard to the subject matter covered. It is sold, or otherwise provided, with the understanding that the publisher is not engaged in rendering professional services. If professional advice or other expert assistance is required, the services of a competent professional should be sought.

The statements and opinions contained in this book are strictly those of the author(s) and do not represent the official positions of the American College of the Healthcare Executives or of the Foundation of the American College of Healthcare Executives.

06 05 04 03 02   5 4 3 2 1

Library of Congress Cataloging-in-Publication Data

Laubach, Christopher L.
    Mastering the negotiation process : a practical guide for the healthcare executive / Christopher L. Laubach.
    p. cm.
    ISBN 1-56793-170-7 (alk. paper)
    1. Health services administration. 2. Health service administrators.
    3. Labor contract.
    I. Title.

    RA 971.3 .L357 2002
    362.1'068'4—dc21

                                                          2001051517

The paper used in this publication meets the minimum requirements of American National Standard for Information Sciences—Permanence of Paper for Printed Library Materials, ANSI Z39.48-1984. ∞ ™

Acquisitions Editor: Marcy McKay; Project Manager: Helen-Joy Bechtle; Cover/Text Design: Matthew T. Avery; Cover photo: Digital Imagery © copyright 2002 PhotoDisc, Inc.

Health Administration Press
A division of the Foundation of the
  American College of Healthcare Executives
1 North Franklin Street, Suite 1700
Chicago, IL 60606-3491
(312) 424-2800

CONTENTS

This book is dedicated
to my father, Peter,
a patient father,
a wonderful teacher,
and a masterful negotiator.

Foreword

THE ABILITY TO negotiate effectively is a requisite for modern life. Whether the bargaining dynamic involves a teenager trying to obtain the keys to the family car, a kindergarten student angling for a trip to an ice cream parlor, or a debate on a fair rate for reimbursement of healthcare services, fair and effective negotiating can ensure that disparate interests can be blended into an outcome that is acceptable, and hopefully favorable, to all parties concerned.

In the arena of healthcare leadership, the art and science of negotiation is required in almost every situation. Indeed, the healthcare leader's charter is to synergistically combine the talents, ideas, and performance of highly skilled, very intelligent individuals into a focused fusion of effort and efficient delivery of services. Large staff populations such as nursing compete for budget dollars against "smaller" units, such as diagnostic services and the hospital pharmacy, that still need resources and hold equilibrate value to the organization. Financial quagmires must be negotiated with the proper blend of courage and consideration, while reimbursement issues are an omnipresent challenge for the healthcare leader at every level. The time-honored tradition of "dealing with the docs"—also known perhaps more euphemistically as physician relations—is a responsibility that must be undertaken and negotiated on an everyday basis, in some regard, by the progressive healthcare leader.

The importance of these responsibilities mandate strategies—more powerful in scope and depth than the pop psychology tomes that all too often are granted a biblical reverence by business leaders. Whether the objective of these volumes is defined with metaphors of attempting to reach the "yeszone" or determining where someone's cheese was moved, these quick-fix concepts in negotiation might have some surface relevance for a healthcare leader and a concomitant short-term benefit, but do not offer the range and regard for specific approaches needed daily in healthcare. The healthcare leader must find a well-calibrated set of strategies aimed at achieving mutually beneficial, long-term agreements.

This book offers the specific, relevant methods needed by the healthcare leader given the particular nuances of the healthcare forum. Based on a pedagogy that has proven its merit over the past 20 years in American College of Healthcare Executive seminars and other summit forums, the strategies delineated in this text by their creator, Chris Laubach, provide immediate effectiveness and improved negotiation dexterity. Presented in a user-friendly, common-sense fashion, this book will provide you with a very practical text that will act as a real-world resource from the commencement of your reading and, moreover, to the first time you experience the success garnered from the implementation of its ideas.

The non-psycho-babble delineation of the material in this book allows you to absorb the essence of negotiation as it applies to the variety of your daily accountabilities. The field-proven strategies will resonate with you as they are specifically tailored to the situations, individuals, and entities you encounter in your very unique workplace. Fully illustrated with examples—not unattainable paradigms—the text provides both the insight and scope of understanding vital to ensuring that its context is readily adaptable. It has equal value as a daily guide for improving your skills in this area as well as a teaching tool for those you mentor and guide through the various quagmires of mixed interests and assorted agendas. This book will help you navigate all of those conundrums toward benefits that enhance patient care and work-life quality for those selflessly dedicated to the healing process.

Keep an open mind and clear perspective as you turn the pages— you are about to learn an array of valuable lessons that will, in short summary, make your life easier while improving the efficacy of your leadership efforts.

Donald N. Lombardi, Ph.D.
Seton Hall University
June, 2001

Preface

NEGOTIATING SUCCESSFUL agreements in today's healthcare environment presents a formidable challenge for healthcare executives. In a world of managed care, hospital-physician integration, and multi-institutional mergers, members of the healthcare profession are faced with creating agreements in which the complex services of healthcare can be delivered in a coordinated and financially viable fashion. To meet this challenge, healthcare executives must develop negotiating skills that can achieve mutually beneficial, value-adding agreements. This negotiating ability will largely determine the future success or failure for many healthcare individuals and organizations.

Mastering the Negotiation Process: A Practical Guide for the Healthcare Executive is intended to help the reader negotiate successful agreements in this challenging environment. With practical approaches and proven negotiating techniques, this book will serve as a handy reference on approaches and strategies used by successful negotiators throughout the industry. Although the book is supportive of contemporary theories, its goal is to give the reader practical and easily understandable techniques and tactics that can be used in the everyday work environment.

Chapter 1, "Negotiating in the Healthcare Environment," discusses the importance of negotiating successful agreements for today's healthcare organizations. The chapter also reviews the history of healthcare negotiations and the challenges faced at today's bargaining table.

Chapter 2, "Approaches to Negotiation," examines three common approaches to a negotiation—logical, threats and intimidation, and psychological. The advantages and disadvantages of each approach is analyzed, and suggestions are made for effectively combining them in the negotiation process.

Developing a fundamental understanding of the basic process of negotiation is broken down into two chapters. The first of these, entitled "Prenegotiation Preparation Phase," (Chapter 3) examines issues and ideas that should be addressed before sitting down at the bargaining table. "Formal Negotiation Phase" (Chapter 4) examines the strategies and approaches used in an actual negotiation.

Using the basic process as a foundation, "Optimizing the Negotiation Process" (Chapter 5) examines the concept of interest-based negotiating and its use in healthcare situations. Looking at negotiations ranging from one-time, short-term transactional bargaining through long-term, mutually beneficial relational negotiations, the reader will gain an understanding of how to apply various strategies and techniques. Also examined are the ways in which negotiations can be kept on the "high road."

Chapter 6, "Negotiating Techniques," presents time-tested techniques that are applicable in any negotiation situation. How and when to use these techniques, including how to deal with an opponent's techniques, is the focus of this chapter.

"Common Negotiating Situations" (Chapter 7) presents suggestions for handling issues that are specific to three-way negotiations, telephone negotiations, and monopoly or sole-source scenarios.

Chapter 8, "Challenging Negotiating Situations," offers practical solutions for dealing with tough negotiations, managing the inevitable conflict in negotiations, dealing with "non-negotiators," and handling negotiators who resort to "hardball" negotiating techniques.

The final chapter, "Becoming a Masterful Negotiator," looks at the personal characteristics of top negotiators and suggests ways in which you can adapt your negotiating style to emulate them.

Mastering the Negotiation Process: A Practical Guide for the Healthcare Executive is a valuable resource for readers who wish to further develop their negotiating strategies and techniques. As a guide to negotiating successful agreements, it serves as a reference for understanding the framework for the negotiating process, as a handbook for understanding negotiating techniques, and as an illustrative text for applying these ideas in the challenging healthcare environment.

Acknowledgments

A WORK OF this kind is the result of more than one individual's efforts. Everything in this book is the result of somebody else's thoughts and ideas, support, or assistance. I owe particular thanks to the following:

To the thousands of healthcare executives who have allowed me to participate in or observe a wide variety of healthcare negotiations over the past two decades, thank you for sharing your ideas, experiences, wisdom, and friendship. Without learning from these many unnamed individuals, it would be impossible to present many of the practical ideas in this book.

To my wonderful wife, Nancy, who patiently waits back home while her husband is on another road trip. Her unwavering support has helped me through lonely times in strange cities, flight delays, and the challenges of being a "not-always-home" father to our wonderful son.

To the education division of the American College of Healthcare Executives for its continuing support in offering our negotiation seminars to its members. For almost 30 years, we have enjoyed a mutually beneficial, interest-based relationship.

To Marcy McKay, and the entire staff at Health Administration Press, for putting forth an exemplary and totally professional effort. Without their expertise, support, and deadlines, it is doubtful this book would have ever developed into a useful text.

CHAPTER 1

Negotiating in the Healthcare Environment

HEALTHCARE IN THE new millennium is an industry marked by fierce competition, decreasing resources, alternative delivery systems, and calls for increased quality and accountability. Hospitals are faced with declining inpatient volumes and are looking at new programs and services to make up for lost revenues. Physicians are constantly threatened with loss of control or autonomy in addition to suffering continuous erosion in income levels. Managed care organizations must compete for members in a marketplace saturated with competitors. The "golden era of healthcare," if it ever existed, has certainly passed.

In this environment, organizations and individuals are challenged on a daily basis to provide high-quality services in a coordinated and financially viable manner. To succeed in this arena, parties need to work with one another under agreements reached through the process of negotiation. Physicians and hospitals need to work hand in hand to develop coordinated, high-quality care that delivers the maximum value for the scarce healthcare service dollar. Providers and health plans need to cooperate to deliver their product to members demanding higher levels of clinical outcomes and customer service. People in healthcare continually negotiate agreements with coworkers, customers, suppliers, regulatory agencies, and a host of other parties. The healthcare industry's success will be attributable in large part to the establishment of agreements satisfying the objectives, interests, and desires of all parties involved.

The process of negotiation usually brings to mind two parties reaching an agreement on a contract or the price of a product or service. However, a multitude of other negotiation situations exist where parties must successfully negotiate the implementation of collaborative working relationships between departmental personnel, establish integration between two merged entities, create risk-sharing ventures between insurers and providers, or create affiliations among industry participants. These are simply a few examples of the types of negotiations that a healthcare manager must successfully resolve on a daily basis. In all these situations, the participants seek a resolution that works for both parties, can be successfully implemented, and that will continue to be effective in the constantly changing healthcare environment. Throughout the text, the term "opponent" is used to designate the person(s) you are trying to convince of the merits of your position. In this context, "opponent" should not imply an adversarial relationship.

The successfully negotiated agreement is not simply about achieving monetary gains, favorable resource allocations, or gaining control over another party. The key measures of a truly successful agreement are that it achieves the desired results, satisfies the interests of all parties, can be implemented and administered easily, and leads to a mutually beneficial, long-term relationship. An organization that negotiates an agreement that is forced on the opponent and simply creates immediate gains for the organization will seldom survive in today's healthcare environment.

HISTORY OF HEALTHCARE NEGOTIATIONS

For most of the past century, healthcare negotiations took place on a simple "transactional" basis. Negotiating the purchase of a piece of equipment, rates with a local insurance company, a collective bar- ~~*TRANSACTIONAL NEGOS - simpler times*~~

gaining agreement with a labor union, or a certificate of need application with a planning agency were typical situations. The negotiations led to a form of bargaining that was straightforward with
a limited purpose, scope, and duration. The negotiations were resolved in a manner similar to what a person might experience in purchasing a car from a local automobile dealer. After some limited discussion about facts and issues, the negotiation eventually became a
session of give-and-take bargaining or haggling. The outcomes of
these negotiations were largely determined by factors including the
relative bargaining power of the two parties, the superior use of facts
or knowledge, and the tenacity of a particular negotiator. Less competition and greater resource availability also affected the negotiations. For instance, in the era of cost plus reimbursement, negotiations between a buyer and a supplier were very different from the
negotiations that take place today.

Although many of these transactional negotiations still occur,
other types of negotiating situations and approaches have emerged.
As the healthcare industry has become more complicated, the complexity of the negotiations have also increased. Changing delivery
methods, increased entrepreneurial activity, evolving regulatory environments, and changing reimbursement methodologies have raised
the stakes at the bargaining table. Compounding the situation is the
growing realization of the "interdependency" among industry participants and the complex cause-and-effect relationships that result
from negotiated agreements.

NEW CHALLENGES IN HEALTHCARE NEGOTIATIONS

In conducting these "new era" negotiations, the parties must now
have a clear understanding of an agreement's objectives or vision,
establish realistic expectations for each party, agree on means or
methods to accomplish the objectives, and establish effective accountability with its attendant risks and rewards. Provider affiliation

agreements are good examples of negotiations in which participants must agree on where they want to go, how they will get there, and what happens if they either succeed or fail. Failure to negotiate an agreement that addresses all of these areas will usually end up with a less than optimum result. In some cases, the affiliation will fail to achieve its desired result because the objectives were not clearly defined or one party's needs went unmet because the interests were not clearly understood by both parties. Sometimes, confusion or disagreement occur during the implementation of the agreement as some guidelines were omitted or not aligned in the direction of the desired results. Finally, a lack of accountability may not properly motivate one of the parties to perform under the agreement.

Today's healthcare agreements must also possess greater flexibility as the assumptions and promises on which they were established are constantly bombarded by changes in a competitive, evolving marketplace. A return to the bargaining table shortly after reaching an agreement may not be unusual because the parties have uncovered new information, a competitor has redirected its strategies, or marketplace demands have changed. In other cases, your new partner may have altered his or her positions or interests. Whatever the case, adjustments will be necessary to ensure that the agreement reflects the changes that have taken place. Although most parties will return to the table to make adjustments, one party who may have felt unfairly treated in the initial negotiation may now view the existing agreement as favorable. Keep in mind during these "relational" negotiations that the relationship you establish with the other party during the negotiation may be more important than the specific agreement that is reached at the bargaining table.

Today's negotiating environments are certainly more susceptible to higher levels of conflict. Some of the sources of conflict are declining resources, loss of income, increased competition, differing values, fear, stress, and the simple effect of change. In negotiating successfully today, the healthcare executive must be prepared to identify sources of conflict, prevent its escalation, and, when possible, redirect it in a productive direction.

The evolution of the healthcare marketplace has led to an evolution in negotiating successful agreements. Where at one time a hard-nosed, tenacious bargainer might succeed, today's negotiator must be prepared to take a new approach in constructing the complex agreements that will serve all parties' interests in a mutually beneficial manner.

MASTERING THE NEGOTIATING PROCESS

Becoming a masterful negotiator is well within the reach of any healthcare executive. Negotiation has no secrets, no special techniques or "silver bullet" that is universally effective. Negotiation is an entirely learnable process. As the healthcare executive goes through the process multiple times and becomes comfortable with its application, the negotiation outcomes will improve. By understanding the process and its various steps, the executive will find that arriving at a resolution that satisfies all parties may be accomplished.

It is not enough, however, to just understand the process of negotiation. To suggest that a "cookbook approach" could be used in all situations would be misleading. Just as a baker will adjust a recipe for different types of flour, ovens, and altitudes, the negotiator must adapt the negotiation process for the particular circumstances encountered. Understanding relative bargaining power, the nature of the agreement, and the opponent's expectations are all factors that must be considered when modifying the basic process of negotiation.

Within the overall process are a number of other issues and ideas that a masterful negotiator considers. Various decisions, analyses, process steps, and optimization techniques, as presented in Figure 1.1, need to be considered and used where appropriate. Approaching the negotiation in a thoughtful and diligent manner will yield the optimized negotiated agreement that the masterful negotiator seeks.

Masterful negotiators also possess certain personal characteristics that affect their success at the bargaining table. Traits such as

Figure 1.1: The Path to an Optimized Negotiation

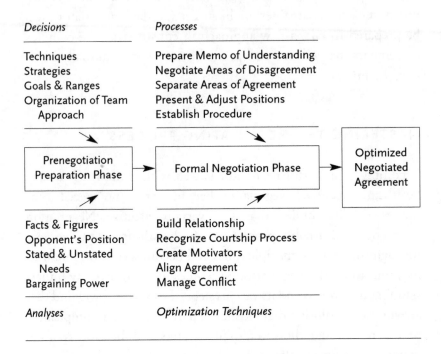

Decisions

Techniques
Strategies
Goals & Ranges
Organization of Team
Approach

Processes

Prepare Memo of Understanding
Negotiate Areas of Disagreement
Separate Areas of Agreement
Present & Adjust Positions
Establish Procedure

Prenegotiation Preparation Phase → Formal Negotiation Phase → Optimized Negotiated Agreement

Facts & Figures
Opponent's Position
Stated & Unstated Needs
Bargaining Power

Build Relationship
Recognize Courtship Process
Create Motivators
Align Agreement
Manage Conflict

Analyses

Optimization Techniques

superior listening skills, honesty and integrity, an "abundance" mentality, a sense of fairness, and a "systems" orientation are some of these qualities. Strong interpersonal skills are also a characteristic of the successful negotiator. Adopting the characteristics of the masterful negotiator and developing a better understanding of the negotiation process will not only help to successfully reach agreements in today's healthcare environment, but will make negotiating an exciting and rewarding experience.

CHAPTER 2

Approaches to Negotiation

CONCEPTUALLY, DIFFERENT approaches or schools of thought about how to negotiate a successful agreement abound. Various books on the subject suggest distinct ways a party may persuade an opponent of the merits of his or her position and achieve a desired outcome. Your own experiences would further suggest that no two parties approach the negotiating table in exactly the same fashion or employ the same strategies and techniques. The fact is, there are as many ways to negotiate as there are negotiators.

However, considering the myriad ways in which people may negotiate, it is possible to distill down these various approaches and find three fundamental ways to reach an agreement at the bargaining table. The first is the use of logic as the basis for one's negotiating position. A second approach is the use of threats or intimidation as a means to force an opponent to accept one party's position. Finally, a third approach involves using psychological techniques in a manner that consciously, or quite often subconsciously, changes the opponent's mind on a particular position. Commonly, in real life negotiations, a combination of these approaches is used. The combination that is used may be based on the negotiator's style, the particular opponent, or the nature of the negotiation itself.

Although all of these approaches can be effective, recognizing the proper use of each approach as well as their advantages and disadvantages is important. A good negotiator will also understand how to handle situations where one or more of these approaches is used by an opponent and how best to deal with the approach to your advantage.

Logic-based negotiating serves as the foundation of the skilled negotiator's approach in any negotiation situation. The goal is to reach a workable agreement using logical positions and arguments. Logic is the simplest negotiation approach and provides the best defensive position when a negotiator encounters an opponent using other approaches such as threats or intimidation. This approach will be discussed in detail after the threatening and psychological approaches.

THE THREATENING OR INTIMIDATION APPROACH

Threats or intimidation is one approach a negotiator may encounter. Using the threat of competition or a deadline may often be necessary to influence the opponent. However, while this approach can be effective in some situations, a negotiator must be careful how and when it is used. Consider your own reactions when someone seeks to reach an agreement by using "pressure tactics" or "take it or leave it" positions. Using this approach as your primary means of reaching an agreement is probably not desirable in most negotiating situations.

The difficulties of using threats and intimidation in a negotiation are threefold. The first problem is the type of agreements that result when someone uses this approach. Typically, the negotiator using threats or intimidation is only concerned with getting what the negotiator wants in an agreement with little or no consideration of what the opponent's needs might be. In these take it or leave it situations, the resulting agreements tend to be one-sided and fail to make logical sense for both parties.

The second problem in using this approach is the damage it does to the relationship between the parties. When one party is subjected to threats and intimidation, he or she will be less likely to do business with the other individual or organization in the future. Given that most negotiations in the healthcare industry are with opponents with whom you will wish to continue doing business, it is extremely important to give due consideration to "relationship management." Many negotiators summarize their feelings after being subjected to this approach as, "I want revenge." A person may get even by either subverting the current agreement or by striking back in a future negotiation. While it has been suggested that this technique could be used in a one-time negotiation situation with another party, it should be remembered that the bad feelings created at the negotiating table could carry over into the implementation of the agreement.

Finally, threats and intimidation cannot always be used in negotiations. For this approach to succeed, the party must possess vastly superior bargaining power over the opponent. For example, an insurer who is the marketshare leader might make use of this approach in negotiating rates with a particular provider, while the provider could not use a similar strategy with the insurer. One problem with taking advantage of a superior bargaining position in such a manner is that bargaining power tends to shift over time. A good example of this situation was the threatening approach used by several health maintenance organizations (HMOs) during the 1980s and 1990s in a time when they possessed superior bargaining power. Using a heavy-handed, threatening approach, these HMOs were able to extract significant discounts from providers. In the last several years, however, providers have experienced growing bargaining power and are now looking to get even. In fact, many of the HMOs who used this "pillage and plunder" approach are now finding few providers willing to work cooperatively with them, and some have even been forced out of the business.

To avoid the problems of this approach, a wise negotiator will use a threat with a logical foundation. Introducing the fact that you can purchase a similar product from a competitor for less cost is a common, logical threat. Presenting the need to reach an agreement prior to a deadline imposed by a regulatory agency is another example. Using a threat or imposing a deadline in situations such as these can be an effective secondary approach in the negotiations while the negotiator concentrates on using logic as the primary approach.

THE PSYCHOLOGICAL APPROACH

The use of psychology to change an opponent's position or way of thinking to reach agreement is the third fundamental approach in negotiations. The methods used in this approach range from soft, fuzzy techniques to some that are rather bizarre.

Examples of the soft, fuzzy techniques are creating a "win-win" situation or meeting an opponent's unstated needs. Emphasizing the mutual interest of both parties in reaching agreement and seeking a solution whereby both parties can gain by reaching an agreement is both a logical goal and a psychologically pleasing outcome. However, creating a situation where both parties can "win" seems both mutually exclusive and contrary to logic. This is not to say that a goal of "win-win" is not appealing, but rather the accomplishment of a "win-win" may be difficult. Also, in every negotiation an opponent will have both stated needs, reflected in their positions or opening offer, as well as unstated needs. Both types of needs will need to be satisfied if an effective resolution is to be reached. However, a concession made to an unstated need will not be given its proper value simply because an opponent has never expressed a desire for the concession. A better approach, using logic, is to ask questions that will reveal the opponent's unstated needs. When the opponent's unstated needs are "stated," making the same concession regarding the unstated need will allow the negotiator to seek something in return.

More radical psychological techniques have been endorsed by some experts in the field. These techniques are used to distract, intimidate, confuse, or send subliminal messages to a negotiating opponent. For example, the use of a mirrored wall in a conference room where an opponent is forced to sit facing the wall can be very distracting as he or she sees themselves talking. Having a bizarre painting on the wall of the place of the negotiation, or simply turning down the thermostat are other examples designed to confuse or distract an opponent. Breaking an opponent's concentration may cause mistakes due to lack of focus.

The problem with these extreme measures is that they result in difficulties similar to those created by threats and intimidation. First, if the techniques have been successful, the agreement reached will usually not reflect an agreement that is logical for both parties. Similarly, if the approach has been successful, the opponent will eventually recognize what has occurred and the relationship between the parties will be damaged.

A psychological approach can also be difficult and ineffective. For example, in a technique called psycholinguistic negotiating, one negotiator is listening for keywords and phrases used by an opponent as a way to discover the "hidden meaning" behind the opponent's words. The difficulty with this approach is that during the heat of a negotiation it is hard to determine what key phrases or words to listen for and then determine what those words or phrases are supposed to mean. Also, many skilled negotiators may send misinformation either intentionally or unintentionally through the use of certain language or phrases. Similarly, reading body language during negotiations can also be difficult and misleading. Although it is true that you may determine your opponent's feelings to some extent through body language, some negotiators who understand these techniques will send other messages or misinformation.

Another problem with using psychology as a core approach in negotiation is its relative effectiveness with different negotiating opponents. Although it may be easy to break the concentration of some negotiating opponents, the same techniques used on an individual who is prepared with strong logical support will not be as effective, if at all.

The wiser approach is to use psychology to augment a logical approach. One example where psychology can be used effectively to increase bargaining power is with a negotiating team rather than a single individual. Experience has shown that negotiators will attribute greater bargaining power to a well-unified negotiating team than they will to a single individual, even when both are holding the exact same position. When dealing with an individual, the perceived challenge is to convince a single individual of the merits of your position. When facing a group, however, a negotiator will feel the need to convince or persuade multiple persons to get the same agreement. Due to the perceived challenge in convincing a team, the negotiator will attribute greater bargaining power to this opponent.

Negotiating Versus Haggling

Another way to look at negotiations is to understand different philosophies regarding how a negotiation is conducted. One approach is simple positional bargaining, or haggling. With this philosophy, both parties simply assume starting positions and begin to trade positions back and forth with no real rhyme or reason behind the positions. Such would be the case in negotiating the price of art objects with an antique dealer or in arriving at the price of a used car. Little or no logic supports the positions, but rather they rely on a series of give and takes based on emotions, patience, threats, and so forth until the two parties reach a point that is agreeable to both.

Another philosophy that is often used is one of principled bargaining as described by Roger Fisher and William Ury (1981) in their book, *Getting to Yes*. The idea behind principled negotiation is to address the issues that separate the two parties and that have resulted in their different positions. Their approach is to resolve the issue based on objective, agreeable principles. One example of this would be the negotiation of a performance-based incentive program that would adjust the compensation to employees based on the achievement of defined goals and objectives. Which philosophy is best? Most negotiations are resolved using a combination of both philosophies with principled bargaining used where possible and any remaining issues settled through positional bargaining. For example, in managed care negotiations, issues related to medical management, marketing, and patient satisfaction are often dealt with in a principled fashion with the final agreements over reimbursement rates settled in more of a "haggling" environment.

In determining which negotiation approach to take, the skilled negotiator will try to predict how the opponent may negotiate. Conducting a principled negotiation will be difficult if the opponent is using positional bargaining supported with threats and intimidation. In the negotiation theory of the "lowest common denominator," the negotiator must always be prepared to match the opponent's approach or at the least have a good logical stance on which to defend his or her positions. Although this is an unfortunate situation for a negotiator, it would be unwise to expose your own position in a more collaborative, principled approach only to find the opponent using your information solely as a means to get a greater gain for the opponent's side.

THE LOGICAL APPROACH

Using a logical approach in negotiations involves two basic principles. The first principle is that any agreement reached must make logical sense for both parties. A good agreement must be acceptable to both parties and it must be able to be implemented without undue difficulty. Although the primary concern in any negotiation is to obtain an agreement that makes logical sense for the negotiator's organization, the negotiator must consider whether an agreement makes logical sense from the opponent's position. If the agreement does not makes sense for the opponent, approval or ratification from the opponent's organization will be difficult. Further negotiations could be required and delay the finality of an agreement (not to mention the probability that the negotiator may have to make further concessions to win agreement from the opponent's organization). More importantly, if an opponent makes a mistake and agrees to an illogical outcome, implementation of the agreement will be difficult, if not impossible. A negotiated agreement is the beginning of the deal, not the end.

For example, in the healthcare industry some managed care contracts contain terms and conditions that are not workable or feasible. These "gotcha clauses," often inserted in fine print deep in the contract, involve burdensome tasks for the practitioner relating to such issues as medical management or reimbursement, and second opinion or pre-authorization requirements. In many cases, practitioners have signed these agreements without sufficient thought or consideration of the implications of these terms and conditions. Later, after realizing the onerous terms they have agreed to, practitioners may use creative ways to avoid or subvert the clauses such as changing a diagnosis. In fact, a recent survey by the American Medical Association found that a majority of its members admitted to having misled a payer at one time or another. It could be reasonably assumed that a number of the "untruths" were simply a way for the provider to "wiggle" out of an illogical situation they had found themselves in due to these contract terms.

The second principle of the logical approach to negotiation is that the negotiator should make use of logic whenever possible in presenting positions, making arguments, or offering concessions. The negotiator should point out facts or figures, industry standards, regulatory limitations, policy constraints, and the like, that support the negotiator's positions. Why use logic? Simply put, a logical position will be the most difficult one for the opponent to assail and gives the negotiator a firm foundation on which to establish positions and arguments. Conversely, if an illogical, arbitrary, or emotional position is taken, a skilled opponent will simply ask a few

Figure 2.1: Range of Settlement

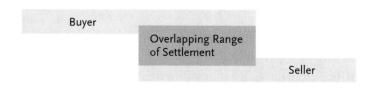

questions and the negotiator will inevitably have to move to a position that can be logically supported.

Seeking out logic and recognizing where it can be used will be a major effort during the prenegotiation preparation phase (see Chapter 3). Interestingly, when one party has not developed a logical position from which to negotiate, that party may only be left with threats and intimidation or psychology.

The Logical Approach Process

In a straightforward economic negotiation such as purchasing an automobile or piece of capital equipment, a negotiator can begin to understand how a logical approach in negotiation works. The buyer and seller each has a range of settlement on the price they would be willing to pay or receive for the negotiated item (see Figure 2.1). For the seller, the range has a maximum price at one end; at the other end of the range is the minimum amount the seller would be willing to accept before walking away from the potential sale. Similarly, a buyer has a starting price and a maximum limit on price. At any point where these two ranges overlap can an agreement be reached. When using a logical approach to negotiation, the negotiator needs to develop a range of settlement as well as ascertain, or at least estimate, the range of settlement of the opponent. The negotiator's job will be to engage in the negotiation process until reaching a point in the overlap, preferably toward the negotiator's favored end.

However, some negotiations have no overlap in the range of settlement and an agreement that makes logical sense for both parties cannot be reached. Many may opine that the current situation in the Middle East reflects a negotiation with no overlap and any agreement between the parties is difficult to imagine.

Both parties approach negotions with a range of acceptable values, not simply a single point. An inexperienced negotiator often believes in some "magic" point at which both parties should agree. In truth, many points exist at which both parties may feel that an agreement will make logical sense. In these situations, the unskilled negotiator becomes willing to accept the first counteroffer made by an opponent that falls within the overlapping range of settlement. For example, a supplier who offers a price within the buyer's budget might be quickly accepted by the buyer, even though further concessions can and should be sought.

The Seller's Range of Settlement

By asking certain questions and applying some basic economic thinking, a seller's range of settlement in an economic negotiation can potentially be determined prior to the negotiation. In determining the high-end of the range of settlement, a buyer could ask for an opening offer from the prospective seller. The opening offer may be in the form of a proposal, the published price list, or in the case of an automobile, the manufacturer's sticker price.

The opening offer is simply the maximum price a seller would expect to get. In reality sellers are typically willing to accept something less. For most people, common sense dictates that in purchasing an automobile or a house, the seller's opening offer is merely a starting point for bargaining. In other situations, such as when purchasing an appliance or clothing from a department store, many people improperly assume the store expects the opening offer to be accepted. Assumptions like these have prevented many negotiations from ever taking place.

Is there a rule about when an opening offer can or cannot be negotiated? Absolutely not. Some will say anything is negotiable, which is understandably not true. On the other hand, unless an opening offer is challenged, whether it can be negotiated will never be known. Challenging an opening offer may be uncomfortable for some people, while others are worried that the challenge may damage a relationship or be culturally unacceptable. On the other hand, in negotiations outside of the United States, many cultures expect the opening offer to be challenged and are disappointed if it is not. Skilled negotiators never assume that the opponent expects the opening offer to be accepted and will at all times challenge this opening position.

At the other end of a seller's range of settlement is the lowest position the party will go to consummate a logical agreement. Using basic pricing theory models from microeconomics, the end of the range of settlement for a seller may be based on cost, competition, or market factors.

Cost-based pricing suggests that a seller will not go below the seller's cost, plus a reasonable profit, to make a sale. Doing so would certainly put the seller out of business in the long term. Managed care contracts are a good example of where selling below cost has occurred in healthcare. For many years, providers were willing to sell to managed care organizations at prices below cost to preserve patient volumes. The economic shortfall of such pricing was "cost shifted" to other patients where reimbursement greatly exceeded cost. As managed care grew to an increasing percentage of the payer mix, many providers found it difficult to continue to shifts costs to the few remaining "charge paying" patients. This "lose money on every patient but make it up on market share" pricing philosophy has resulted in economic distress for many healthcare providers today. While cost-based pricing may represent a clear theoretical low for a seller, other factors must be considered to maximize profitability in the organization's negotiation outcomes.

In a competition-based pricing model, a seller will go no lower than slightly below the seller's nearest competitor. For example, if other medical equipment manufacturers are offering a product at no lower than one million dollars, a supplier will not go much below $999,999, even if the supplier's costs are only $800,000. As a negotiating strategy, a buyer will use multiple rounds of negotiations with several competitors in an attempt to get them to "leapfrog" one another to win the contract. Each supplier, on the other hand, will want the "last look" at the deal and attempt to beat out the best of the competitors' offers.

Finally, in situations with little or no competition, a seller will consider pricing its product at a price the "market will bear." Drug manufacturers with the only product of its type on the market can often charge significant amounts for that product. When purchasing the "latest and hottest" automobile on the market, a buyer will often pay the full sticker amount, or more, where demand exceeds supply. In a monopolistic situation, a seller has no incentive to go any lower than the maximum the seller believes the buyer is willing to pay.

The Buyer's Range of Settlement

As a buyer in an economic negotiation, the opening offer represents the starting point for bargaining. This point needs to be low enough to give the parties room to negotiate but not so low as to appear unreasonable. The starting point is not arbitrary but rather one that can be supported from a logical standpoint. One way to determine a reasonable starting price position when purchasing a new product is to reference the prices of the same used product with a small adjustment reflecting the added value of a new unit. Although a seller may not accept this opening position, it gives the buyer a range to make further concessions while at the same time extracting further concessions from the seller.

The other end of the range of settlement, or walk-away point for any buyer, is often established on an approved budgeted amount. For example, an individual from New York City might establish the maximum he or she is willing to pay for an automobile at a price equal to what it would cost to use public transportation and rent cars when necessary (minus the cost of parking and insurance).

Another way to look at the end of the range of settlement for both a buyer and a seller is to consider the alternative scenario if the negotiation fails. This concept, which Fisher and Ury term the "best alternative to a negotiated agreement" (BATNA), suggests that each party consider the next best, or fall back, situation if the negotiation is unsuccessful (Fisher and Ury 1981). For a seller this may mean "a half a loaf is better to no loaf at all." For the buyer, the BATNA in acquiring new equipment might be to look at higher priced alternatives, lost market opportunities if the equipment is not purchased, or lost productivity and higher costs from using the current, outdated equipment. Any buyer who has ever been told that "this is a once in a lifetime opportunity that will never come again" is often being sold with this concept.

In a recent example, a medical center's construction claims case involved an amount of approximately $75,000. For quite some time, the parties were unable to negotiate an agreement and the potential for a lengthy arbitration case grew. When both sides were presented with the fact that the legal expenses of going to arbitration (the BATNA) to settle the dispute would exceed the $75,000, the parties quickly saw it was in both of their best interest to resolve the case without the involvement of attorneys.

Obviously, establishing ranges of settlement for buyers and sellers is easier in a simple economic negotiation. In more complicated negotiations, however, many issues to be resolved are not as easily quantifiable—issues such as medical management disputes or negotiation over issues of control, egos, or power. This is not to say that establishing a range of settlement in such situations is impossible; the challenge is to estimate or create reasonable and flexible ranges of settlement for both parties. In the following chapter on the prenegotiation phase, further discussion of ranges of settlement and how they may be developed will be discussed.

REFERENCE

Fisher, R., and W. Ury. 1981. *Getting to Yes: Negotiating Agreements Without Giving In.* New York: Penguin Books.

CHAPTER 3

Prenegotiation
Preparation Phase

WHEN PREPARING TO engage in a logical approach to negotiation, the negotiator must develop a strong sense of reality for both parties. Reality is the underlying focus and driving force of almost every negotiation. The negotiator's efforts in creating and presenting an accurate interpretation of reality that is supportable with logic is essential for convincing the opponent of the reasonableness of any agreement. In every negotiation, each party will arrive at the table with his or her own perceptions of the situation, interpretations of the facts, and assessment of what is important. Each party will sincerely believe that his or her analysis of the situation correctly reflects the reality of the situation. Both parties will feel correct in their assumptions of where things are and how things should change. The fundamental issue in a negotiation will then become, *whose reality is going to prevail?*

In every negotiating situation, each party will present its position and its assessment of reality. The negotiator's ability to support his or her position with information, and the manner in which that information is presented, will determine the negotiator's ability to persuade the opponent to agree with his or her vision. During the prenegotiation preparation phase the negotiator has the opportunity to assess the situation from both parties' perspective, establish the arguments and counterarguments that may be used in justifying a position or moving the opponent off of his or her position, and recommend ideas that will satisfy the needs and interests of both parties in a logical, workable agreement.

A survey of professional negotiators found that seasoned negotiating experts spend between 85 and 99 percent of their efforts or time in any negotiation preparing for the formal negotiating phase. Consider, for instance, how many governmental analysts and strategists work around the clock to prepare the U. S. Secretary of State for a three- or four-hour negotiation with a foreign government. Thousands of hours of behind-the-scenes efforts are usually involved. In your own experience, can you recall entering into a negotiation without adequately preparing and encountering a well-prepared opponent? Do you recall the outcome? It was probably less than satisfactory. On the other hand, think of the negotiation where you were well-prepared and met an unprepared opponent. The results were probably very different and much more in your favor. In the same survey, the professional negotiators also estimated that 75 to 85 percent of the outcome of a negotiation was determined by activities that took place prior to the actual initiation of the formal negotiation. In other words, in the minds of the experts, a negotiator's ability to influence the outcome once the formal negotiations have begun is quite limited—in the range of 15 to 25 percent.

At a negotiating seminar I once attended, the speaker, a nationally recognized negotiator, related a simple poker game analogy to demonstrate the importance of prenegotiation preparation. He first proposed a situation in which a person was sitting at a poker table playing five-card draw and was dealt four aces. In this case, he suggested, the outcome would almost certainly be in the cardholder's favor and his or her face-to-face poker-playing skills would not be very helpful. He then suggested a second situation where the same person was dealt five cards that were "pure junk." In that instance, he proposed that even if the cardholder had great poker skills and a convincing "poker face," anyone at the table who decided to stay in the hand and call the cardholder's bluff would eventually win. At this point he asked the audience the question, "But what is the key difference between playing poker and negotiating?" His answer was that when you play poker, the cards are dealt facedown so the hand you receive is decided by pure chance. In a negotiation, however, you have the opportunity to deal your own hand and increase your chances of winning by dealing yourself the best hand available. He further stated that during the prenegotiation preparation phase you have the best opportunity to deal yourself a good hand or a bad hand. Finally, he completed the point by suggesting that even if you never improve your face-to-face negotiation skills used during the formal negotiation phase, you can still improve the likelihood of getting a better outcome simply by dealing yourself the best hand possible.

How do you improve your negotiating position during the prenegotiation preparation phase? Factors include choosing the right negotiator or negotiating team, identifying needs, establishing goals and ranges of settlement, obtaining approvals for negotiating positions, and using time to your advantage. Other factors to be discussed include evaluating your opponent's possible strategies, developing strategies you expect to follow during the negotiation itself, and testing your strategies and positions prior to the formal negotiation phase.

ASSEMBLING THE NEGOTIATORS

The first step in prenegotiation preparation is to identify the individual or team that will represent the organization as its negotiator(s). In a simple, transactional negotiation, a single individual who possesses the requisite negotiating skills and subject knowledge will be best. In negotiations that are more complex and involve difficult clinical, financial, or legal issues, or where the agreement may affect a large number of parties, using a negotiating team may be preferable. In other cases, the best alternative may be to employ an outside negotiating agent. All of these approaches have advantages and disadvantages that should be carefully considered.

Team Negotiations

As the nature of healthcare negotiations have become more complex, the conditions for using negotiating teams is more often justified. Negotiating teams have a number of advantages. First, they allow the negotiators to bring the necessary expertise to the table. People with expertise in areas of clinical knowledge, financial acumen, or legal counsel may all need to be present. Individuals with talents in these areas are invaluable both in preparing for the negotiation as well as providing on-the-spot support when these subjects are brought up at the bargaining table.

Negotiating teams also provide an opportunity for better listening. During a negotiation most individuals have a tendency to begin preparing a response to the opponent's statement before the opponent has finished talking. While effective listening is a hallmark of the skilled negotiator, listening effectively is difficult when you are also the one responsible for providing the response to the opponent's statements. The individual tends to listen to the opponent make a point or two and then shift thinking into "rebuttal mode," thereby failing to hear the remainder of the statement. A negotiating team can be particularly effective if one member is assigned the task of observing the opponent without being responsible for actually responding to the opponent's statements.

Moral support is another benefit to using a negotiating team. In any negotiation the opponent will be taking a position other than your own. When a negotiator is alone, an element of self-doubt can creep into the negotiator's thinking, particularly when faced with an articulate, logic-based opponent. However, after a team has prepared and agreed on the logic of the team's position, a single negotiator will have the confidence to stick to the position longer.

Sometimes a negotiating team may be necessary to gain cooperation and "buy in" to an agreement. Agreements can affect a number of different departments or organizational entities and quite often each party will want its own representative to look out for its interests.

A negotiating team also affords the negotiators the opportunity to caucus during the course of the negotiation. By simply stating to the opponent "that is an interesting fact we had not considered, could you please give us a short period to discuss it among ourselves," the team has the ability to adjust strategies or develop arguments before proceeding with a negotiation. Another benefit of using a negotiating team is that it allows for role playing. For example, the finance person may take a heavy-handed approach with a capital equipment supplier, while the end user or department head can take on a more congenial tone. This strategy allows the end user to maintain the positive relationship with the supplier that will be necessary during the implementation of the agreement and continued use of the equipment.

Finally, and most importantly, a negotiating team is often more successful due to the simple fact that the members are usually better prepared. When a busy healthcare professional is approaching a negotiation alone, the professional will often find that there are other pressing matters that require immediate attention. Unfortunately, these interruptions do not allow the negotiator to adequately prepare. On the other hand, negotiating teams seem to recognize that they must get their act together before the negotiation, and will place a higher priority on getting together to prepare for the negotiation. Because of this better preparation, it often seems that negotiating teams achieve better outcomes.

Proper Use of a Negotiating Team

Whenever a team of individuals is used to negotiate, it must be recognized that the team is composed of individuals each with their own biases and ideas about what they wish to achieve. A team leader must be chosen to mediate disagreements among members, consolidate opinions into a solidified position, and unify the group. Additionally, the leader should be a strong negotiator familiar with the needs, goals, and expectations of the organization. Without a strong leader, the team can fall apart and work at cross-purposes if faced with a skillful opponent. During the negotiation itself, the team leader should be the primary spokesperson and all other members of the team must honor this position and speak only when recognized by the spokesperson. This "team discipline" is often difficult to maintain, but in situations where everyone on the team speaks, a skillful opponent will simply focus on the team member who appears to be the weakest negotiator or the member most sympathetic to the opponent's position.

Simply sending a number of individuals to the negotiating table does not necessarily represent effective negotiating team strategy. Teams must include individuals who will contribute to the prenegotiation preparation phase and be ready to participate when called on during the negotiation. Although it is sometimes necessary to use team members whose busy schedules do not allow their participation in the prenegotiation preparation meetings, such as with a private practicing physician, this may result in situations where a dispute will arise among the team at the negotiating table in full view of the opponent.

The size of a negotiating team is another factor that must be considered. While a large team might be desirable in terms of moral support or a "show of strength" to the opponent, a cohesive team position may be difficult to maintain. Generally, more than five team members makes it very difficult to maintain discipline, and the benefits of additional team members is questionable. Personal experience suggests a team of three members is an ideal number that gives most of the benefits in using team negotiating while also facilitating communication and coordination among members.

For example, a proposed provider agreement was being negotiated that affected approximately 25 physicians or medical groups.

Rather than sending a representative from each group to the negotiations, the group chose to conduct a "sequential" negotiation among themselves prior to the actual negotiation for the agreement. At this private negotiation, the various groups negotiated the goals, strategies, and positions the smaller negotiating team would be authorized to seek at the bargaining table.

Using a negotiating team is not always appropriate. Situations that are limited in scope or would have minor economic impact would not justify using scarce resources for a negotiating team. In other instances, showing up with a large negotiating team when dealing with a single individual, such as a physician, may be perceived by the individual as an attempt at intimidation and could result in derailing a logical approach to resolving the situation.

Negotiation Agents

In some situations, using an individual or a negotiating team from the organization may not be the best approach, rather, handing over the negotiation to an outside agent may be best. The negotiating agent is one who not only has the requisite knowledge of the subject being negotiated, but also has superior skills as a negotiator. For example, it is not uncommon to find hospitals and other organizations engaging negotiating experts in labor relations to handle union negotiations, or health systems using negotiating experts in information technology as consultants to negotiate the acquisition of a new information system.

A common strategy in using a negotiating agent is sending an agent to the bargaining table with limited authority, thus forcing an opponent to make one-way concessions when faced with an agent whose hands are tied. Finally, even if an agreement is reached by an agent, the organization will still have the right to review the agreement and, if desirable, to negotiate further. Using an agent with limited authority has been a common tactic in many negotiations.

Using an agent may backfire, however, when an opponent may refuse to negotiate when he or she finds that the agent does not have the authority to consummate an agreement or is severely limited in bargaining beyond certain limits. The opponent may also counter by employing an agent as well.

SETTING NEGOTIATION GOALS

Before beginning any negotiation, goals must be set. The organization must be fully aware of what it plans to attain at the negotiating table. At this time, the organization should decide on lofty goals, set priorities for those goals, and enter the negotiation with a high level of expectation. Also, obtaining approval for the planned actions from a higher level of management or from the parties who will be affected by the ultimate agreement is desirable.

Determining Negotiating Needs

It is mandatory during prenegotiation preparation to identify the organization's specific needs. These needs can be expressed in terms of specifications (written or drawn), services, alternatives, revenues, salaries, operating costs, time schedules, location, contract terms and conditions, and so on. If needs are not expressed in specific terms, the negotiator's ability to prepare for the negotiation and to conduct the negotiation itself is severely limited. If you were to walk onto a car dealer's lot and simply state, "I need a new automobile," your outcome will likely be determined by what the dealer wants to sell (or dump) on you. On the other hand, if you have an idea of the model, color, accessories, financing terms, and warranty requirements, your likelihood of getting the exact car you want will be much improved.

The negotiating team leader should make every effort to identify specific needs. The team leader will often discuss these needs with members of the medical staff, trustees, sales and implementation teams, network development staff, and provider relations superiors. The inability to identify specific needs will result in a less than concrete agreement and one that may be subject to many changes. Also, if any members of the organization have unrealistic or unnecessary needs, they will need to be adjusted prior to developing the team's position.

Levels of Expectation

What makes one negotiator more successful than another in terms of results? The answer may be their respective levels of expectation. One study of federal government buyers showed that those negotiators who expected more (i.e., lower prices, better delivery, etc.) tended to get more. Your own experiences in bargaining could probably verify this study if you have ever purchased a house, car, or other big-ticket item. For instance, if the asking price on a house is $250,000, you could offer $240,000 and possibly split the difference at $245,000. On the other hand, you might be able to justify an initial offer of $200,000 based on the location of the home, comparable houses, or other supportable reasons. By doing so, you might ultimately get the house for substantially less than $245,000 or $250,000. Or you may exact other concessions from the seller such as favorable payment terms, repairs and upgrades, or appliances.

The reasons that high levels of expectation are so important are twofold. First is the simple fact that if you aim higher, you tend to hit the target higher. More importantly, a high level of expectation will have the immediate, psychological effect of lowering the expectation level of the opponent. You may have encountered a situation, similar to the one illustrated in Figure 3.1, in which a buyer had established a range of settlement of between $75 and $125 for a particular item. Based on the buyer's prenegotiation preparation work, the buyer may have expected the seller to begin with an offer of around $150, and eventually go as low as $100. The buyer may

Figure 3.1: Effects of High Expectations

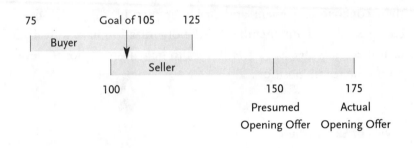

have set the ultimate goal for his or her negotiation at a point around $105, which would represent a good outcome. When the buyer gets to the negotiating table, the opponent makes an initial offer of $175 rather than the $150 as expected. What immediately runs through the buyer's mind? It is likely that the buyer instantly forgets about the goal of $105 and instead expects that he or she will have to work simply to get the opponent back to $125. In this situation, the buyer reduced his or her level of expectation simply because the opponent came in with a very high level of expectation.

When is the best time to communicate a high level of expectation? The single best chance is probably in the opening offer, as seen in Figure 3.1. The opponent will probably be unaware of your position and therefore will be more open to having his or her expectation levels changed. Another good opportunity to communicate high levels of expectation will be with the size and timing of the first concession in a negotiation. Negotiating with an opponent who does not make any concessions for a long time and then finally—and begrudgingly—makes a small concession might make a negotiator think that the negotiation will take forever and that the negotiator will not get much out of the opponent. On the other hand, if the opponent makes a quick and large concession from the initial position, the negotiator's level of expectation probably increases as the negotiator believes the opponent may come all the way to the negotiator's position with little further effort or time.

Many negotiators, however, fail to use the opportunity to communicate high levels of expectation due to fear that it will result in a deadlock. Although this is certainly a risk when holding high expectations, both parties in a negotiation stand to gain through the results. Consequently, deadlocks or a failure to come to any agreement are not that common. However, the negotiator must have a reasonable level of support for their opening position. When purchasing an automobile, it is not reasonable to walk onto the lot and tell the salesperson that you want the car for free as your opening position. The salesperson would simply walk away and seek other customers who were being realistic. As an alternative, you might show up with a classified advertisement for a used vehicle of the same make and model being sold by a private party. Because the private party is selling a slightly used car at a price below what the dealer's price is likely to be, this would be an effective, reasonable, and supportable opening offer. Although you will not get the car from the dealer at the same price as from the private party, you have given yourself some room to begin the negotiation.

Perception of Value

When discussing goals and levels of expectation, consider the question of value. The only way a negotiator's position can be justified is when the opponent's perception of value is in line with the negotiator's position. Value is in the eye of the beholder, and a negotiator's position and persuasive arguments should support the opponent's perceptions of value. In healthcare negotiations, the question of value is often raised in terms of adequate reimbursement for physician services, the purchase price for capital equipment, or an appropriate salary for an employee. Often independent information is available to establish value. A physician's compensation may be valued by using a resource-based relative value scale (RBRVS). When establishing a purchase price for capital equipment, a competitor's price or a life cycle value analysis might be performed. Salary surveys are commonly used to establish appropriate salary levels for individuals in an organization.

However, in some situations, establishing value may be more difficult because little or no frame of reference is available. During the years of frenzied acquisitions of physician practices, the value of a practice was different for several acquiring parties. For example, a hospital might be willing to pay for hard assets and a small amount for goodwill, while a physician practice management company saw greater value in the goodwill of the practice and was often willing to pay two or three times the amount offered by the hospital. When establishing goals and levels of expectation, keep in mind the idea of value as perceived by your opponent.

Another important step in assessing value from the opponent's perspective is to perform a self-assessment of your current position and worth. While it is important in any negotiation to support your value based on your strengths, recognize where your weaknesses exist in your opponent's eyes. For example, an academic medical center may perceive its reputation as a center of excellence as a "value enhancing" asset, thus increasing its value to a managed care organization. From the managed care organization's perspective, however, this reputation might serve as a catalyst for adverse selection, thereby driving up its medical costs and actually reducing the value of having this provider in its network.

Acknowledgment of Strengths and Weaknesses

Acknowledging and addressing your weaknesses as well as your strengths is critical prior to any negotiation. If the negotiator avoids or pretends that weaknesses do not exist, the negotiator will lose the trust and respect of the opponent. If, on the other hand, the negotiator understand his or her weaknesses, the negotiator can prepare to deal with those effectively when the opponent brings them up, and, in some cases, turn them to the negotiator's advantage.

For example, turning a weakness into strength was accomplished recently in a negotiation between a medical center and a prospective architectural/engineering firm (A/E firm). The A/E firm knew that the medical center had been in contact with the last healthcare client for which the firm had provided design services. On the prior job a high number of change orders had been initiated by the architect due in part to the complexity of the project and in part to errors made by the firm's design team. The negotiators for the A/E firm anticipated that the medical center would question the A/E firm's capabilities based on information from the other job. When the issue was raised at the bargaining table, the firm quickly admitted to their past history but suggested that they would rather admit to making mistakes then have their reputation tarnished through the delivery of a project to a client that was less than their very best design effort. They also supported the large number of change orders with data from other highly complex design projects that were similar in size and scope. By admitting to their past mistakes, the firm not only increased their credibility with their new client, but they also created an expectation that some level of architectural errors are inevitable and, therefore, allowable in the contract.

The Purpose of Setting Goals

Negotiation goals are the product of your needs and levels of expectation. Goals should reflect the organization's sense of reality supported by sound, logical arguments, and should also push the limits of what can be expected in the negotiation. If your need is for a pathologist's services, your goal should reflect a high level of expectation. For example, the negotiator might propose to a pathologist that he or she accept a straight salary comparable to that paid to pathologists at a local staff-model HMO. The negotiator might also propose that for this salary the pathologist would be expected to spend a certain number of hours a week serving as an educator and as director of the hospital's quality assurance program. In another example, a hospital was interested in acquiring a new piece of monitoring equipment from a company whose manufacturing plant was located in the same town. While the hospital had a need for the monitoring equipment, the manufacturer wanted to use the hospital as a showroom for potential clients where they could combine site visits for both the clinical setting as well as the manufacturing plant. In approaching the manufacturer, the hospital not only asked for the equipment at cost, but also asked for free maintenance and upgrades during the life of the equipment. The hospital suggested that since the hospital was the "showroom," it was in the manufacturer's interests to have the most up-to-date equipment in proper working order at all times. Further, the hospital asked to be paid a token fee for each site visit to the hospital to cover expenses incurred by having its clinical personnel escort guests and explain their experiences with the equipment to the potential clients. Did they get everything they asked for? No, but they purchased the equipment at 10 percent over cost and received free maintenance and upgrades for five years. Was this a high level of expectation? You bet! As is often stated in the world of negotiation, "you never know until you ask." Goals can be lowered later in a negotiation, but seldom can they be raised.

Obtaining Authorization for Positions

In any negotiation that involves large sums of money or highly technical products, that has a potentially significant effect on the organization's future strategies or operation, or in which the agreement may affect multiple parties, the negotiator should have the negotiation positions reviewed and approved by a higher level of authority within the management structure (e.g., the hospital, CEO, or trustees). Not only should senior management or the board be fully aware of the negotiating position in advance, but they should review and approve the limits or ranges of settlement established by the negotiating team. If the team hits the limits authorized, then the senior management or board can decide whether to change the limit or terminate the negotiation. Where a negotiation involves less significant items, the negotiator should have limits in terms of committing the institution. For example, a hospital purchasing agent might be limited to committing the hospital to purchases of up to $50,000 and only for items on the approved capital or operating budgets.

Closely related to the preceding point is the "limitation of authority" concept. In most cases, the negotiator or negotiating team should not be authorized to commit the institution at the negotiating table. Any agreements reached should be subject to ratification by a higher level of management or by the board. By being limited in the ability to commit, the negotiator can use the higher authority as an excuse to delay the negotiations, seek further concessions, or avoid making additional concessions when being subjected to high-pressure "closing" techniques by an opponent.

UNDERSTANDING YOUR OPPONENT

Once the organization's own positions, ranges of settlement, and so on, are understood, it is then time to develop an understanding of the opponent's position. The negotiator must conduct research to understand the opponent's business, industry and market forces, stated and unstated needs, the composition of the negotiating team, possible strategies and techniques, and the decision-making process the opposing organization will use in ratifying an agreement. By gaining an understanding in these areas, the negotiator will be better prepared to create a logical agreement for both sides, effectively deal with the personalities and strategies encountered at the negotiating table, and streamline the process for ultimately reaching agreement.

Understanding Your Opponent's Business and Market Forces

One of the keys to reaching better agreements comes with knowing what the opponent's business is all about. Developing sound arguments, making meaningful concessions, and reaching logical agreements are all affected by the opponent's business perspective.

In my work with both provider organizations and managed care organizations, I have witnessed a general lack of understanding by each party of what the other's business entails. The managed care organizations fail to recognize the challenges faced by providers in delivering quality healthcare with a customer service orientation. On the other hand, providers fail to recognize that health plans look at their business as a "numbers" game and will manage their products, populations, and providers according to the data they collect. I was once told by a CEO of a large integrated delivery system that the single biggest barrier to truly integrating the delivery and financing elements of the health system was that the two divisions did not understand each other's business needs and requirements.

Knowledge of the market forces exerted on an opponent is important in preparing for a negotiation. If the negotiation is with a pharmaceutical supplier who has the latest wonder drug on the market without any competitors, its team will negotiate very differently than a supplier that faces significant competition for market share. Similarly, a new managed care entrant into an existing, well-developed market will negotiate with providers very differently than a well-established player with significant market share.

Analyzing Your Opponent's Position

The opponent's stated goals are those contained in his or her proposal. Some proposals may be elaborate written documents while others may be simple oral requests. In all instances, a thorough analysis of the proposal will augment the negotiator's bargaining position. The first step in analyzing a proposal is to determine if the organization's specific needs are met in relation to what the proposal offers. With a carefully drafted request for proposal (RFP), an organization may receive proposals that meet its exact specifications. In other instances, the supplier may offer an alternative. In these cases the organization may have to bring in experts to evaluate the alternative in relation to its needs. These experts may consist of clinical personnel, attorneys, financial experts, or others.

When analyzing proposals, the organization should also relate the price being proposed to the value of the item being procured. The term "value added" is often offered by sellers as one of the attractive benefits of their proposal. It is important, however, to recognize whether it represents true value to the organization or is simply an unnecessary bell or whistle. Asking for a guarantee or a risk-sharing provision involving these value-adding features will often expose the validity of the seller's promises.

In addition to value analysis, a cost analysis might be prepared, and certainly should be prepared on any high-dollar procurement. This may require no more than a simple analysis of competing or "going" rates. In securing consulting services, it is not difficult to determine what rates for similar services are being offered in the marketplace. For capital equipment purchases, the use of the services of equipment database companies such as MDB Information Network (formerly MD Buyline) or ECRI may be useful.

However, should the situation warrant, an in-depth evaluation of the elements of cost in a proposal may be required including analyzing proposed labor hours, labor rates, material costs, overhead rates, profit margins, and other factors. For example, in securing the services of an architectural/engineering firm, you might request a breakdown of hours by personnel type, rates by personnel type, hours estimated to complete the design by personnel type, hourly rate multipliers in their breakdown, and, finally, profit. This breakdown can be further segmented by the phases of design such as schematic design, design development, and construction documents.

Your Opponent's Terms and Conditions

One final step in proposal analysis is an examination of the opponent's suggested terms and conditions. An old purchasing axiom says, "Unless you get what you want, when you want it, price is irrelevant." In other words, while the price of a product is of paramount importance, other specifications and terms and conditions must be considered. Terms and conditions should be examined carefully in relation to the organization's needs and the reasonableness of the terms. Virtually every term and condition of a proposal is subject to negotiation. However, in many situations, an opponent will argue that certain conditions are "company policy" and cannot be changed. In most cases, this is a smoke screen and the policy could be challenged if it is in the negotiator's best interests to do so. Only where federal, state, or local laws mandate terms and conditions are they generally not subject to negotiation.

Fact-Finding

During the prenegotiation phase on a complex proposal, the negotiator may find it desirable to have a formal face-to-face fact-finding session with the opponent after submission of the initial proposal. During this fact-finding session, the negotiator's objective will be to completely understand the proposal, clarify specifications, proposed costs, and so on. At the same time, the negotiator may want to further explain the organization's needs and requirements to allow the opponent to refocus the offer. On less complicated negotiations, fact-finding may involve simply writing a letter asking for clarification on points made in the initial proposal.

A seller may also want to seek out the buyer's position. While it is usually the seller who is forced to submit an initial proposal, there are opportunities to examine a buyer's position prior to the negotiation. For example, a hospital may be "selling" a state-planning agency on the need for a new cancer treatment center on its campus. By talking to agency officials, the seller could discover the methodologies, assumptions, and policies related to how the buyer will analyze an application. This information would then be valuable when sitting down at the table to negotiate a final agreement.

Understanding Your Opponent's Unstated Needs

The opponent's stated goals or needs can be ascertained from the proposal (or from the analysis of the proposal in situations where you may be submitting the initial offer); however, consideration must also be given to the opponent's unstated needs. Every individual has certain fundamental behavioral needs such as recognition, security, acceptance, and a feeling of importance. A skilled negotiator's prenegotiation preparation will include consideration of the opponent's unstated needs, because concessions to those needs will likely have to be made and can strongly influence the outcome of the negotiation. In fact, meeting the opponent's unstated needs will often be the "clincher" in obtaining an agreement, and these concessions frequently cost little or nothing to make. On the other hand, not meeting an opponent's unstated needs will often result in personal conflicts, walkouts, or no agreement at all.

For example, in a recent negotiation between a medical center and an information technology (IT) supplier, the issue of unstated needs was quite apparent. The medical center had engaged the services of an IT consultant to help in the negotiations, serving as its expert in IT. During the course of the negotiations, the consultant made several recommendations to the medical center for changing the proposed system or improving the terms of the agreement. These ideas were consistently downplayed or outright refuted by the supplier's representatives. While the supplier's proposal was the most attractive to the medical center, the consultant refused to endorse a decision to award the contract to this company. Finally, the IT supplier recognized that one unstated need for the consultant was to look good in front of the client. At the next negotiation meeting, the supplier not only agreed to some of the consultant's recommendations but also let the medical center representatives know how creative and invaluable those ideas were for them. After finally getting the recognition the consultant desired for serving the client's needs, the consultant endorsed the proposed agreement.

Once a negotiator has determined the opponent's unstated needs, the negotiator should consider ways to get those needs stated. This often difficult step is important because a concession to an unstated need is also a concession that was never requested. On the surface, therefore, the concession carries little significance and will not get much in return. On the other hand, if the negotiator can find a way to have an opponent identify his or her unstated needs and then make the exact same concession, the negotiator will be in a position to ask for a similar concession from the negotiator's side.

Analyzing Your Opponent's Negotiating Team

A careful analysis of your negotiating opponent is the next step in the prenegotiation process. The opponent may be a single individual or a team. To better understand the opponent's needs and probable positions, it is necessary to see the world through the opponent's eyes, and understand how he or she thinks, feels, and what the opponent cares about. Never underestimate the opponent's ability to completely justify in his or her mind a position you may consider irrational or preposterous. Rather than simply dismissing such positions as unrealistic or unjustifiable, consider the position from the opponent's viewpoint and begin developing effective arguments that will convince the opponent to shift views.

When dealing with a negotiating team, remember that the team is nothing more than a collection of individuals with their own perspectives, ambitions, and expectations. While the negotiator will need to spend more time investigating the personal characteristics of each team member, an analysis of an ominous-looking negotiating team will usually reveal some of their weaknesses. During your career, you have probably found yourself repeatedly negotiating with the same opposing negotiating teams. After some time it becomes apparent which of these people are cooperative in negotiations and which are difficult. Some will frequently identify with your positions while others will constantly challenge them. Those who may be sympathetic to your side and those who are diametrically opposed are probably not the people on which to concentrate your negotiating efforts. Rather, the "swing people" ordinarily decide what to do about a proposal. Effective handling of these individuals will be a significant factor in your success.

Another way to analyze the opponent's team comes from Stephen Heiman and Diane Sanchez in *The New Strategic Selling*, where the authors look at the buying influences of potential customers (Heiman and Sanchez 1995). The authors define a "coach" and three types of buyers; an economic buyer, a user buyer, and a technical buyer. The economic buyer's primary focus is on the cost or price of the proposal. A user buyer's attention is on how the product or service will benefit his or her department. The technical buyer is concerned with the terms and conditions of the proposal and whether the proposed agreement can be implemented within the organization. Finally, a coach is someone who can help the seller navigate through the proposal and negotiation process as a form of a mentor. When you analyze an opponent's negotiating team, look for these characteristics among the team members and identify which obstacles must be overcome and from where you may get support.

For negotiations with new opponents, find out how they have behaved during other negotiation sessions. You may want to interview your colleagues who have dealt with them in the past and talk to people who may appear on a client list.

Analyzing Your Opponent's Past Strategies and Techniques

Although past behavior does not guarantee how a person will act in a subsequent negotiation, past performance can be fairly predictive and will provide the negotiator with some insight into what type of negotiator the opponent is and what the negotiator might encounter at the negotiating table. If possible, analyze what the opponent has done successfully in the past and where he or she has proved vulnerable. If a union has used walkouts in the past as leverage to acquire concessions and the strategy has worked, the union will probably try it again. If an opponent has imposed deadlines to force an agreement and was successful, the opponent may try this strategy again. If an opponent has tended to wander from the subject in the negotiations or has confused the issues, he or she may do so again. Consider developing a strategy for this type of opponent that will keep him or her on the topic, such as using an agenda. Similarly, if an opponent's concession patterns seem to accelerate as a deadline approaches, the negotiator may wish to forestall large concessions early in the negotiation as a possible strategy.

Based on the opponent's past track record, the negotiator can select the approach best suited to the situation. Be prepared to handle the opponent's best strategies and exploit the weak ones, recognizing, however, that any assumptions about the opponent's past behavior are just that—assumptions. If the opponent is a skilled negotiator, he or she may totally change approaches in the forthcoming negotiation. Therefore, plan negotiation strategy assuming the opponent will behave as he or she has in the past, but recognize that the opponent might totally change his or her approach this time around. In a similar manner, the negotiator should evaluate his or her past negotiating methods and behavior. Doing so may reveal distinguishable patterns on which the opponent might capitalize.

For example, the salespeople for a large equipment supplier were making large concessions close to the deadline to meet their individual sales quotas. Their potential customers usually knew of these quarterly deadlines as well as the behavior of the salespeople and used these predictable behaviors to their advantage. The company realized that this pattern of behavior was being exploited and the pressure of the deadlines needed to be reduced or eliminated. By changing their performance measurement system so that salespeople no longer felt the pressure of these deadlines, the company's negotiation outcomes improved considerably. In summary, avoid predictability whenever possible, yet try to find consistency in your opponent's past behavior.

ANALYZING RELATIVE BARGAINING POWER

Understanding, measuring, and increasing bargaining power is a critical step in the prenegotiation preparation phase. Simply, the more bargaining power the negotiator has, the more influence he or she can exert on the overall outcome of the negotiation. If a negotiator is in a superior bargaining power position relative to the opponent, the negotiator can realistically expect to control much of the agreement. For example, a managed care organization with a 50-percent market share can largely determine the rate it will pay providers as well as other terms and conditions of its provider agreements. Conversely, a provider negotiating with this same managed care organization would not be in a position to demand reimbursement at billed charges or usual, customary, and reasonable rates (UCRs). The skilled negotiator must understand where bargaining power comes from, how to analyze that power relative to the opponent's position, and what steps to take to increase bargaining power.

Bargaining power is always present. The fact that a negotiation is taking place implies that someone has something someone else wants—instant bargaining power. The famous negotiator, Herb Cohen, once said about bargaining power, "If you think you've got it, you've got it. If you don't think you have it, even if you do have it, you don't have it." Bargaining power is based on perception and is almost never one-sided. No one ever has ultimate power, just as no one is ever totally powerless. The seasoned negotiator recognizes his or her bargaining power vis-à-vis that of the opponent and does something about getting more power if not in his or her favor, and uses whatever elements of possessed power to his or her advantage. At the same time, a skilled negotiator will modify strategy depending on the relative strength of the opponent's bargaining power position.

Bargaining power can come in many forms. A world-renowned physician has bargaining power simply by his or her reputation. A CEO has bargaining power with department heads by the very existence of a superior-subordinate relationship. Suppliers may have bargaining power after they have convinced an end user that no suitable substitutes or competitive products meet its needs. In recent years, business coalitions have increased their bargaining power with managed care organizations and healthcare providers because they represent a larger customer base. Also, providers have merged or affiliated themselves with one another in an attempt to increase their bargaining power with buyers of healthcare services by controlling the supply of healthcare services in a given area. However, bargaining power needs to be recognized by the opponent to have the desired effect. In the case of provider mergers or affiliations, some buyers simply short-circuited these "supply side" strategies by going to other providers in the marketplace.

Assessing Bargaining Power

Assessing your relative bargaining strength versus your opponent's should be undertaken in a methodical manner. Unfortunately, many negotiators fail to do this, and in most instances mistakenly attribute greater bargaining power to the opponent. In a superior-subordinate negotiation, most subordinates believe the boss holds all the cards.

On the other hand, the subordinate who has a proven track record and, in effect, makes the boss look good to superiors, is a valuable asset both within the organization and to the boss. If the subordinate were to ask the question, "What happens if I am no longer in my position?" and analyzes the impact upon herself, her boss, and the organization, she will get a much better idea of who might have the real bargaining strength.

Providers almost universally feel that managed care companies have superior bargaining power because of their status as buyers. Managed care personnel, however, usually believe that providers are the ones in a superior position. While a health plan has power as a buyer, without providers the health plan has no network and, therefore, no product to sell. Once again, bargaining power is based on perceptions. The unskilled negotiator who fails to analyze and increase bargaining power will often squander this advantage.

Building Bargaining Power

Opportunities to build bargaining power exist almost entirely during the prenegotiation phase. The negotiator must use this time to think about what steps to take to increase bargaining power. One or more of the following may improve bargaining position.

Knowledge. A negotiator will have an advantage by being familiar with the item or service involved in the negotiation. In negotiating with a physician, a nonclinical person would be at a disadvantage in discussing issues related to clinical guidelines, medical management issues, and so forth. On the other hand, a physician negotiating legal terms and conditions with an attorney would find that the attorney would have the superior bargaining power.

Prenegotiation preparation and negotiation skill. At the beginning of the chapter, the importance of prenegotiation preparation was discussed. The more effort the negotiator puts into preparing support for the organization's position and anticipating the opponent's position, the greater the bargaining power. Anyone who has ever entered a negotiation unprepared and has met a well-prepared opponent recognizes this simple fact. Similarly, the skill you have in negotiating will reflect on your bargaining power.

Use of quantitative analysis and support. Supporting your positions with facts and figures will yield greater power than simply taking arbitrary positions. A thoughtful analysis with sound financial modeling can be quite persuasive at the negotiating table.

Generating competition. One of the simplest and most effective means by which a negotiator can generate bargaining power is by generating competition. Over the years, managed care organizations have been quite successful in using competitive pressures as a means to extract concessions from providers.

Use of bureaucracy, policies, rules, regulations, and budgets. Factual and legal constraints may be used as logical support for the organization's position. The opponent will be challenged to overcome established laws, policies, or budgets with large, powerful entities (e.g., the organization's board, a state regulatory agency). For example, when negotiating with a department head over a request for additional staffing, referring to approved budgets is an effective way to support a firm negotiating position.

Time and patience. Using time effectively is at the heart of any good negotiation. If a negotiator is rushing to reach agreement, the opponent will recognize this and simply wait for the negotiator to make further concessions before reaching an agreement. On the other hand, imposing a deadline on the opponent, or not responding to one imposed on you, can increase bargaining power. Anytime someone is rushing in a negotiation, his or her bargaining power is quickly eroding.

Support of influential people. Having a trustee, a well-recognized member of your medical staff, or high-ranking executive support an issue will often be significant in the eyes of the opponent. Use of these individuals in "backroom" discussions can also often have a major effect on influencing the opponent.

Relations with your opponent. A friendly relationship with the opponent will increase bargaining power, even though the advantage works both ways. If past relations and negotiations have been productive for both sides, both negotiators will feel a commitment to working cooperatively to reach an agreement.

The negotiator's reputation. Being known as an expert, a professional, one who gets things done, or one who makes sure that the agreements work for both parties will enhance your bargaining power.

Firmness. Taking a positive stand with the opponent increases bargaining power. Holding a firm position in negotiations, while increasing the chances for a deadlock, will also tend to lower expectations in the opponent. This is not to say that the negotiator should be abrasive; rather, you should express a resolute attitude in stating positions, issues, or concerns. I often hear negotiators use phrases such as, "we sort of feel" or "we would kind of like" at the bargaining table. While the use of such phrases will certainly not offend the opponent, the phrases represent flexibility in the position of the negotiator. Alternatively, you could say, "we strongly feel" to express the same position. When you later move from that position, it will appear that you have made a larger concession than when you stated "we sort of feel."

These suggestions are just a few of the ways in which negotiators can build bargaining power prior to entering a negotiation. Remember that by increasing your bargaining power relative to your opponent, the outcome of the negotiation will continually move in your favor.

DEVELOPING A GAME PLAN AND NEGOTIATING STRATEGY

Once goals have been established and all necessary information regarding your opponent's possible positions and strategies has been collected, the game plan for the negotiation must be developed. The game plan includes translating goals into ranges of settlement, uncovering the opponent's ranges, identifying areas of agreement and disagreement, preparing arguments supporting your position, developing concession patterns and their timing, deciding on which negotiation techniques will be employed, and preparing an agenda.

Ranges of Settlement

Once goals have been established with high levels of expectation for the negotiation, translate those goals into ranges for settlement. In other words, determine the opening offer and the "walk away" point.

The first purpose of an opening offer is that it must reflect a high level of expectation. The second purpose is that it must generate a counteroffer, or in other words, start the negotiation process. Consider, however, that these two aspects of a strong opening offer run somewhat counter to one another. With too high a level of expectation, the opponent may simply walk away from the bargaining table. On the other hand, if the opening offer is so low that it is guaranteed to be attractive to the opponent, an opportunity has been lost to communicate a high level of expectation. In the worst case, these "safe" opening offers may actually be accepted. In balancing these two purposes, the opening offer needs to be a carefully thought-out position that can be supported by fact and logic while at the same time present as high a level of expectation as the opponent can tolerate. It does not have to be the most supportable position but simply one that has a basis in logic. The question I often hear from people is, "How far can I push my opening offer before they will walk away?" I often respond with the question, "How many instances have you experienced where someone has walked away from your opening offer?" In most cases, people will say no one has ever walked away from their opening offers. I then suggest to them that they keep pushing their levels of expectation higher until someone does finally walk away. At that point you will know you have gone too far and it is time to back off.

Equally important as the opening offer is the other end of the range of settlement. This end of the range, often referred to as a walk-away point, needs to be carefully established. This point may be represented by a budgeted amount, a cost limitation, a limit dictated by organizational policies, or the point at which the agreement no longer makes logical sense. Your best alternative to a negotiated agreement (BATNA) may be another method to determine this end of the range of settlement. Why is it so important to establish this end on your range of settlement? If you have ever looked at buying a house and have fallen in love with a particular home before negotiating its price, then you may know the answer. The result is that you probably paid too much. Why does this happen? Psychologically you have a personal and/or a business interest in reaching an agreement, so you simply continue to negotiate and make concessions until an agreement is reached. Unless you have established an end to your range of settlement, you will negotiate beyond the point at which you should have walked away.

Uncovering Your Opponent's Range of Settlement

During prenegotiation preparation, an attempt should be made to determine the opponent's ranges of settlement. In many cases, the opponent's proposal will contain the high end of the range of settlement. Typically, however, the low limit will not have been exposed. A negotiator may be able to get an idea of what this lower limit might be by conducting a detailed cost analysis that may uncover areas that contain "fat" or other nonessential items. An analysis of proposed terms and conditions may indicate items open to revision such as payment or delivery terms. Comparing prices from competing suppliers or substitute products may indicate how low a seller might go, and discussions with other clients may reveal the degree to which a supplier has lowered its limits in other situations. Further, a negotiator may get some insight into the opponent's maximum limits by examining published data such as plans or budgets, detailed proposal review standards, or screening criteria.

For example, the process of developing capital equipment budgets at hospitals often involves requesting a quotation from a potential supplier. This quoted figure from the supplier, which is often close to list price, will quite commonly become the hospital's budgeted amount. In such a situation, is not difficult for the sales representative to know exactly what the hospital's upper limit is for the purchase. Compounding this unfortunate situation for the hospital is that, in many cases, the department head or end user involved in the negotiation will translate the budgeted number, which is simply the maximum amount that can be paid, into the negotiation goal.

Arguments and Counterarguments

A confident, well-prepared negotiator will have developed, in advance, supportable positions with strong arguments. Successful negotiations are dependent on supportable high and low positions. When possible, the position should be supported with quantitative data that will be hard to dispute. When a position is supported in numerical terms, bargaining power is enhanced. A department head requesting pay raises for her staff would find it difficult to argue against going rates and fringes for comparable work in the service area. Negotiating with physicians over their excess utilization of resources will be much easier if they are provided with data showing their performance relative to their colleagues or other established standards. A physician once told me, "Whenever you are negotiating with physicians, if you have to use words, then you are in trouble."

He was relating the fact that physicians are data driven. By providing good comparative data, a negotiator stands a much better chance of having the physicians reexamine their practice patterns, utilization rates, and the like.

Obviously, not everything can be translated into quantitative terms. Supporting quantitatively such things as loyalty, future relations, quality, workmanship, levels of service, and warranties may be difficult. While supporting a position quantitatively is preferable, being able to back the positions with strong arguments and counterarguments in some way or another is always advantageous.

Developing Arguments and Counterarguments

To obtain your goals, strong arguments are needed to support any position. Skilled negotiators provide effective arguments supporting their positions and anticipate, quite rightly, that their opponents will have strong arguments supporting their positions. In other words, both parties believe in their own visions of reality and will have developed strong arguments in support of those visions. The seasoned negotiator, therefore, not only prepares arguments supporting his or her positions, but anticipates the arguments that his or her opponent will be using and prepares effective counterarguments to deal with them. By anticipating your opponent's positions and developing effective counterarguments, you can substantially increase your bargaining power.

Developing strong arguments and counterarguments is one area where attorneys appear to be extremely adept. Perhaps it is because they have become familiar with the adversarial process during their legal training. In the adversarial process, which is quite different than the negotiation process, attorneys try to persuade a judge or jury, not by convincing them of the merits of their client's position, but rather by "destroying" the case presented by their opponent. Their success hinges not on arguing effectively for their client, but rather in anticipating the opponent's arguments and developing strong rebuttals to those arguments. Attorneys are also trained to argue the case for either a plaintiff or a defendant. In this regard, they must be able to argue effectively for whichever side has engaged their services. In preparing for a trip to the bargaining table, seasoned negotiators must think like an attorney and prepare for the arguments and counterarguments that will be presented by both sides.

Order for Presenting Arguments

When, and in what order, should you present your arguments? Some arguments will be more supportable and more effective, while others are weaker. One factor to consider is the recency–primacy effect theory. Psychologists refer to this theory when discussing what people tend to remember. The primacy effect refers to the tendency of people to retain information that is presented to them early in a discussion. In developing a good negotiating strategy, therefore, a negotiator may want to start the presentation with a powerful argument. The recency effect, which is stronger than the primacy effect, refers to the fact that whatever is said last will be best remembered. Consequently, another tactic would be to save the best arguments for last. The weakest arguments should therefore be placed in the middle of the presentation since these will be easily forgotten.

The length of the opponent's attention span may be something to consider when presenting your positions. I have often seen negotiators present long speeches of two or three minutes in duration containing quite a few good arguments. Studies have shown, however, that in negotiations an opponent will listen attentively for no more than 20 or 30 seconds. After that time, the opponent will usually be thinking of his or her responses or rebuttals to the positions and arguments presented in the first few sentences the opponent heard. Anything said after 30 seconds or so will probably not be given full consideration and is therefore wasted. If a statement has several good arguments, a skilled negotiator will consider breaking up the statement into several shorter speeches to get maximum effect from all the arguments.

Identifying Items to Be Settled

During prenegotiation preparation, an all-inclusive list of items to be settled should be developed. "The devil is in the details" when preparing to negotiate. In negotiating agreements relating to information systems, these "issues" lists often run several pages long and include hundreds of items.

At one time or another, every negotiator has reached a tentative agreement with an opponent, usually after settling on the major issues, with the promise that "we will work out the details later." What usually happens with the details? In many cases they become significant issues later and create a scenario where the deal will fall apart. These situations, which I often refer to as "lazy negotiations," usually occur after both parties have invested significant time and emotional effort in reaching an agreement on major issues and are simply too tired to work out the details of the final agreement. However, after a tentative agreement is reached, bargaining power will change. In some cases it may change in your favor, in other cases it will not. Once the seller has a tentative agreement in place, for example, he or she may be less willing to concede on smaller issues related to terms and conditions. The bargaining power of the buyer is greater before the tentative agreement is reached when the buyer has the choice of talking to other potential suppliers and is still in a position to request further concessions from the seller. On the other hand, a seller may want to reach a tentative agreement before negotiating the smaller issues. With competitive pressures removed, and a buyer who may be looking forward to having use of the seller's product or service, the seller's bargaining power has probably increased and the seller will feel less pressure to make concessions to "close" the deal.

Identifying Problem Areas

In any negotiation differences of opinion will arise on such items as price, quality, control, performance specifications, or other terms and conditions. At the same time, there will be many areas of agreement and areas with insignificant differences in position. A negotiator should identify the major areas of disagreement and devote his or her limited time and resources to developing negotiating positions and strategies to resolve these major problems. Where rapid agreement on certain points is obvious, those points should be identified and dispensed with early in the negotiation. Early agreements set a positive tone for the entire negotiation session.

Timing of Offers and Counteroffers

Prenegotiation planning should include consideration of when offers and counteroffers will be made during the negotiation process. Traditional negotiating wisdom was that a negotiator would attempt to get the opponent to make the opening offer in a negotiation. This was based on two factors. First, getting the opponent's position first allowed the negotiator to get a sense of their reality and what issues were of importance to the opponent. Second, by hearing the opponent's position first, the negotiator can avoid an opening offer that exceeds the demands of the opponent.

The buyer is usually in the position of demanding an initial offer from the seller and the buyer will delay the first offer as long as possible while extracting concessions from the seller's opening position. On the other hand, the seller will want to develop a strategy to extract an initial offer from the buyer as quickly as possible.

Are there times when making the opening offer is advantageous? In certain situations, a negotiator may wish to consider making the opening offer even when not required to do so. One reason is that when making an opening offer, a negotiator has the first chance of communicating a high level of expectation and effectively "driving their stake in the ground." By presenting your vision of reality first, you can lower the expectation levels of the opponent and at the same time force them to try to move you off your position. A second reason to consider making the opening offer is to use it as a preemptive strike to prevent the opponent from establishing a high level of expectation. If you believe that you can establish the opponent's range of settlement with some level of certainty, and can justify and support a high level of expectation, then making the opening offer in a negotiation can be a strong offensive strategy. Making the opening offer should therefore be viewed as an opportunity and should be considered during the prenegotiation preparation.

Concession patterns indicate a negotiator's levels of expectation as well. A large, early concession in the negotiation will reflect a low expectation and this, in turn, will tend to increase the levels of expectation by the other party. In terms of concessions or counteroffers, a negotiator generally will want the opponent to make the first concession, hopefully on issues of major importance. This is not to say that a negotiator cannot make small, insignificant concessions to show a spirit of cooperation, but it is usually best to reserve large concessions on significant issues for later in the negotiation process.

Negotiating Techniques to Be Used

The negotiation techniques used to "sell" the organization's position must be considered prior to the formal negotiation. Deciding which techniques to use will be a product of the assumptions made about the opponent's approach to the negotiation, relative bargaining power, expectations, goals, and the negotiator's personal negotiating style. Different techniques and tactics involve the use of questions, role-playing, deadlines, threats, and so on. (Some of these techniques will be explained in more depth in the following chapter.) While the techniques to be used should be agreed on beforehand, be aware that a change may occur during the negotiation if circumstances warrant.

Selecting the Negotiation Site

Some proponents of psychological negotiating suggest it is advantageous to negotiate on your own turf. Controlling the setting, having access to information and subject matter experts, or simply feeling comfortable in your own surroundings are all advantages of this approach. Physical surroundings can provide significant psychological benefits. In many cases, using a conference room where the walls are glass or are mirrored may serve to distract opponents who either have to watch their own reflections or are interested in what is happening outside the conference room. However, at times a negotiator may not want to have access to information (to avoid answering difficult questions), or may want to have limited authority by not having decision makers in the building. In other situations a negotiator will have no choice in the location of the negotiations, such as when negotiating with a public agency. In some situations, a neutral site can be desirable.

Preparing the Negotiation Agenda

Inexperienced negotiators often fail to establish an agenda for the formal negotiation session itself. Many times an unskilled negotiator will simply want to arrive at the bargaining table, deal with the issues requiring resolution in any order, and subsequently reach an agreement. While this may be acceptable for simple negotiations that have a small number of issues, creating and controlling the agenda for the negotiation holds a distinct advantage in most cases. "Writing a script" for the negotiation has several advantages. The first advantage is that all issues to be covered are on the agenda for negotiation. Second, the issues on the agenda can be arranged in such a manner as to achieve quick resolution on issues of less importance while reserving major issues toward the end. Third, an agenda is helpful in dealing with negotiators who tend to stray from the topics at hand and often try to bring in extraneous issues.

Finally, the agenda provides a framework on which the overall agreement can be reached. For instance, in labor negotiations, lesser economic issues are usually discussed early in the negotiation, and wages are one of the final economic terms to be negotiated. By getting a handle on the other economic issues first, employers can look at their budgets for labor and figure out the amount they can put into the basic wage rate.

A written agenda should be provided to the opponent prior to the negotiation. In many cases, the opponent will not have an agenda established and will simply agree to use the proposed agenda. If the opponent does have an agenda, take time to examine it carefully. Pay particular attention to any items they have left off the agenda that are important to you and which you want explored during the negotiation session, that is, certain terms and conditions they may not want to be challenged or that they may not be able to meet, certain product specifications, and so forth.

Testing Your Positions and Negotiating Strategies

After the prenegotiation preparation is complete, a good negotiator will test goals, limits, supporting data, arguments and counterarguments, strategies, and negotiation techniques by using a simulated negotiation or a devil's advocate. Either of these approaches can reveal gaps in positions, prepare the negotiator for potential arguments and techniques by the opponent, and provide a practice session in presenting positions.

The most effective approach in testing a negotiator's position is to engage in a simulated negotiation session. Members of the organization can take on the role of the opponent and engage in a "mock" negotiation to test the negotiator's positions, strategies, and techniques. The most valuable practice negotiations occur when the negotiator has access to an internal resource person who has worked for the other side earlier in his or her career. Managed care organizations often have people who have worked on the provider side for years and use them quite effectively in "acting" as a provider opponent during these sessions.

The other approach that is used quite often is a devil's advocate session. In this approach, your colleagues may ask you every conceivable question about your proposal, its justification, its costs, and its benefits. By raising "what if the opponent says this or says that" questions, they can test your knowledge, arguments, negotiation techniques, and presentation skills.

Both of these methods are designed to determine the answers to the following questions.

- Are goals and expectations too high or too low?
- Are the positions supportable?
- Are the planned arguments strong enough?
- Are all counterarguments prepared?
- Do you have a strong grasp of the opponent's position and are you familiar with how he or she might act?
- Are the negotiation strategies feasible?
- Will you be able to control the negotiation?

If you feel comfortable with your positions and strategies at this point, it is now time to implement your plans in the formal negotiation session.

REFERENCE

Heiman, S. E., and D. Sanchez. 1995. *The New Strategic Selling*. New York: Warner Books.

CHAPTER 4

Formal Negotiation Phase

ONCE YOUR WELL thought out game plan has been prepared during the prenegotiation preparation phase, you are now ready to enter into the formal negotiation session with the opponent. This session will involve (1) agreement on the agenda and procedures, (2) presentation of each party's position, (3) negotiation for agreement, and (4) preparation of the memorandum of understanding.

AGENDA SETTING, PROCEDURES, AND AUTHORITY TO COMMIT

The first step in the formal negotiation process is to reach an agreement on the session's agenda and any special procedures to be used. If you have not presented the opponent with a written agenda yet, it should be the first item introduced at the bargaining table. At the same time, the opponent may wish to propose an agenda, and both parties should compromise on a final plan. Hopefully, the agenda that is finally adopted will enable you to follow through on your strategy. At the beginning of the session, both parties should also discuss procedures such as daily schedules, use of expert testimony, telephone privileges, and so on. Finally, you should also determine whether the opponent has the authority to negotiate and to commit the institution he or she is representing to any agreement worked out at the bargaining table.

Agreeing on an Agenda

Discussing the agenda with the opponent is the first opportunity you will have to determine your opponent's priorities on the issues. The opponent's reaction to the agenda and his or her comments on what issues should be on the agenda will give you some clues about the significance or insignificance of these issues. While not negotiating these issues directly, you can gain a sense of what the opponent believes will be major or minor issues. By understanding the importance your opponent places on various agenda items, you can orient your negotiating efforts to seek concessions in areas of less significance and avoid prolonged conflict over areas that are of greater significance. Also, when discussing agenda items, you might discover those issues that may be the easiest on which both parties will agree. In that case, it may be wise to rearrange the agenda and place such items first on the list of items to be discussed. You create a positive climate by reaching early agreement.

When the parties disagree on certain items to be included on the agenda, you will need to seek an alternative method of establishing which items are scheduled for negotiation and when those topics will be discussed. In some cases, you may decide to have each side propose an issue in alternating fashion until all issues are listed. Another method commonly used is to have one party set the agenda for one day's bargaining session and to allow the other party to set the agenda for the following session. Many other methods can be used, but it is important to not get "hung up" on setting agendas at this point. All points will need to be discussed sooner or later, and creating conflict over setting an agenda is probably not a wise move.

Agreeing on Procedures

In a major negotiation that will take some time to conclude, various procedures should be discussed at the outset. Procedures may include agreements on the schedule, provision of conference room space for each team, the turning off of cellular phones or pagers during negotiations, access to documentation, and so on. Another important procedure item to be resolved is the privilege of bringing resource people with particular expertise into the negotiation itself. Sometimes parties will allow this and sometimes they will not. Procedures should also be established on the use of team subcommittees, such as financial people, to move to another conference room to settle any problems regarding cost or price analyses.

Authority to Commit

The ability of your opponent to commit on behalf of his or her institution is critical and must be determined at the outset of the negotiations. In many instances you will find that the opponent has the authority to reach agreement but must get final approval or ratification from the board, partners, or another senior official. While limited authority in your opponent is not preferable, it is commonplace, and you should not withhold negotiating with such a party. Most healthcare negotiations take place in an environment of limited authority. As long as limited authority is recognized upfront, you can proceed with the knowledge that the opponent has reserved the right to seek final approval outside of the negotiating room. The situation to avoid, however, is dealing with an individual who has little or no room to compromise, as might be the case in dealing with an outside agent representing the opposing institution. Similarly, you want to avoid negotiating with a party who will take up your time examining and bargaining issues, but who says subsequently, "this is a matter you will have to take up with my boss." Another common variation of this type of negotiator is one who, after discussing certain issues, insists these items be discussed by the "legal" department. While a legal review of any agreement is advisable, in many cases the legal department is simply the next level of negotiator from the firm. It is also advisable to walk away from negotiations with individuals who state, "My boss, or my board, will never buy this." Simply tell your opponent that since the boss or board is apparently the one who can commit the organization, you will need to negotiate with that party. You want to avoid being tricked into the old game of negotiating multiple times with escalating levels of authority. Not only is this very time consuming, but it is a ploy effectively used to extract additional concessions each time you move up in your opponent's organization.

PRESENTING EACH PARTY'S POSITION

After the agenda and negotiation procedures have been established, the next step in a formal negotiation phase is for each party to present its position with respect to the items under discussion. At this point, the parties are not negotiating items but simply presenting positions. Presenting positions is a fact-gathering step to allow both parties a chance to understand the other's positions. By listening carefully, you will also have the opportunity to identify the areas of agreement and disagreement.

Following the presentation of positions, it is usually wise to caucus and adjust your negotiating position in line with what you have just heard. Despite diligent preparation efforts, the opponent always brings up unanticipated issues. Before proceeding with the actual negotiation, consider this new information.

The Opponent's Position

The opponent will be presenting the opening offer in the initial presentation, if he or she has not done so already. Remember that this is merely the opponent's *opening offer* and is not expected to be accepted. If the opponent has previously made an opening offer, ask for any modifications or amendments to the initial proposal. Also, be sure the opponent outlines and justifies all positions. If you have questions about the positions or justification for those positions, now is the time to ask. At this stage, you are not bargaining, only gathering facts. You should not be arguing at this point; now is the time to simply listen carefully.

By carefully listening to your opponent and probing with questions, you may be able to gain some additional insights into significant items such as ranges of settlement, areas in which you will have difficulty in obtaining concessions, areas where justification is weak or there is minimum commitment, and the possible techniques and tactics the opponent may use during the negotiations.

Determining Your Opponent's Ranges for Settlement

A successful negotiator is one who will find the opponent's minimum range and attempt to settle the agreement at that level. During your prenegotiation preparation, you estimated the opponent's limits. During the formal negotiation stage, the actual limits might be determined by the following means:

1. Ask your opponent directly what is the best they can do for you. For example, if you are negotiating for the seller ask, "What is the maximum reimbursement your budget will allow?" Whether or not the opponent answers the question is another issue, but it never hurts to ask. If the opponent responds to your questions about limits, you might determine if these are, in fact, real limits by testing with further questions and bargaining.

2. If you are representing the buyer, tell the opponent that your budget does not permit the purchase. At the same time, refuse to reveal the amount budgeted. Ask the opponent what the

bottom-line might be and what concessions the opponent can possibly make. In this manner, the opponent may reveal his or her minimum position.

3. Ask the opponent if a substitute product or service at a lower price is available. You may then attempt to use this price as a limit in obtaining the original product or service.

4. When you are attempting to sell your position, discuss, but do not offer, other alternatives and probe the opponent regarding budget restraints, what the competition may be offering, or what the opponent's limits are.

5. Ask the opponent how much he or she would be willing to concede if you were willing to concede in another area. This sort of "horse trading" could indicate the range of settlement on the issues on which the opponent would be willing to concede. Since you have not made a commitment, you have conceded nothing and have learned something about the opponent's limit.

Presenting Your Position

At this stage of the negotiation, you are still not bargaining but simply presenting your positions. When you make your presentation you will want to let the opponent know what you like or do not like about various aspects of his or her opening offer. The more powerful your presentation, the lower will be the opponent's level of expectations.

The optimal presentation is one that is hard-hitting, direct, and loaded with quantitative and other factual data. Consider arranging your presentation in such a way that your strongest arguments are at the beginning and at the end (recency-primacy effect). Also, present both sides of each issue, anticipating the opponent's arguments and counterarguments. This allows you to control your delivery and present the arguments more favorably to your side. Finally, you may want to raise a large number of issues or points so that the opponent is faced with what appears to be a large gap between the parties' respective positions. Although these issues may not be that important to you, they may come in handy later as concessions that, in essence, have cost you nothing.

Adjusting Your Position

After the parties have both presented their positions, take time to reflect on the information you have received. Even with the most diligent preparation, your opponent may bring up new issues, new facts you had not uncovered previously, possible attempts to build bargaining power through the use of threats, deadlines, and the like. At this point in the negotiation process call a recess so that your negotiating team can reflect on what it has just heard and make the appropriate changes to bargain toward a final agreement. In many situations, this step is omitted and parties simply launch into negotiating an agreement. After weeks or even months of preparation to get to the bargaining table, some people are not willing to take a few extra minutes at this point to ensure a well-reasoned and logical agreement. In many cases the few minutes saved at this stage are spent tenfold more in administering a poorly developed agreement.

During the opening presentation, the opponent may have provided additional information or support for the issues that may bear on the specific arguments you had originally developed during the prenegotiation phase. For example, the opponent may reveal something about the limits that might affect your specific strategy. Similarly, the opponent might provide further information concerning the relative importance of various issues to be resolved. You may consider modifying your approach to avoid taking time trying to get the opponent to concede on issues about which the opponent will take a very strong position. Also, if you find you are going to make a large concession, examining the opponent's total position will be vital in deciding what you will seek in exchange. In some instances, the opponent's presentation will contain points that you had not considered previously. You may be required to seek further consultation with other parties in your organization to gather information, or you may have to go to a higher authority to get their authorization for a modification in your position.

NEGOTIATING FOR AGREEMENT

The most difficult and time-consuming part of the formal negotiation phase is negotiating for an agreement. This is where the action is and also where your preparation and skill in bargaining will pay off. The first step in this procedure is simply to identify and lay aside those items on which both parties agree. Next, on the issues of disagreement, you should attempt to *resolve* the differences so both parties *gain an advantage.* If these issues cannot be resolved, then you will be forced to pursue an agreement through the process of give-and-take bargaining. Finally, a written agreement must be drawn up, reviewed, and approved by both parties.

Setting Aside Agreed Issues

After the opening positions of both parties have been presented, a number of areas on which both parties agree will be apparent. For example, the time schedule or the need for the product or service may not be questioned. Similarly, many terms and conditions may be acceptable to both sides at the outset. Where you find areas of agreement with the opponent, you should note each item and set it aside. Do not waste time discussing these issues further. Rather, spend your time on resolving the areas of disagreement. By setting the initial areas of agreement aside, you also create a favorable atmosphere, signal to the opponent your cooperation, and indicate your desire to reach a favorable resolution on all aspects of the agreement.

Now that the areas of agreement have been set aside, the remaining issues can be worked on.

Sequencing Issues of Disagreement

Several schools of thought exist regarding how the sequence of issues of disagreement should be approached. During your prenegotiation preparation phase, you should have considered whether you want to present major issues of importance up front, or deal with them later in the negotiation. While it is human nature and the tendency of unskilled negotiators to discuss issues of most importance first, this is not always the best way to sequence the negotiations.

Some experts say it is best to deal with major issues toward the end of the negotiation after the opponent has made heavy investments in terms of time and effort to reach an agreement. After working hard to reach agreement on the minor issues, this school of thought suggests that the opponent has become more malleable in his or her attitudes and resoluteness in an effort to close the deal. Additionally, some experts believe that it may be easier to get a handle on the overall agreement once the minor issues have been resolved, allowing the major issues to become more a "plug number." This approach is also recommended in situations where the opponent may be facing a deadline to reach agreement and may give greater concessions as a deadline approaches.

Others experts believe, however, that the major issues should be dealt with up front. Their opinion is that if the major issues cannot be resolved, time and effort is wasted on issues of minor consequence. For example, in a case involving a merger between a Catholic and a non-Catholic institution, reaching an agreement on the issue of providing certain women's services (i.e., abortions) was considered a "deal breaker" by the Catholic institution. Another situation where bringing up the major issues at the outset was critical was in the acquisition of a large group practice by a medical center. The physicians' "deal-breaking" issue was their autonomy and control over the medical practice after the acquisition. Without a satisfactory resolution of this issue, the physicians were not going to agree despite any other favorable agreements on issues of price, ownership of assets, working conditions, and so forth.

One possible rule of thumb regarding the ordering of issues in a negotiation is that if you believe that there is a high likelihood of reaching an agreement, such as in the case of renewing a managed care contract or negotiating a new labor agreement, it may be best to hold off on major issues until the end. On the other hand, if reaching a final agreement is questionable and is hinged directly on a major deal-breaking issue, these matters should be resolved up front before wasting time and effort on less important issues.

Reaching Agreement Through Mutual Problem Solving

In mutual problem solving, the parties attempt to resolve the issues in a manner that is satisfactory to both parties. Mutual problem solving should always take precedence over give-and-take bargaining. For example, during a negotiation between a healthcare system and an information systems vendor, there was a dispute over the schedule of payments for the hardware, software, and implementation fees for the system. The system had concerns over the ability of the vendor to meet the product performance specifications and the project schedule. The system wanted to withhold payment from the vendor until they were satisfied with the performance under the agreement. The information systems vendor, who was somewhat cash strapped at the time, wanted the payment schedule to be accelerated. Eventually, the two parties resolved their differences and addressed each other's concerns through mutual problem solving. How? The vendor offered to accept greater liquidated damages, increased warranty provisions, and a risk-sharing arrangement to guarantee the performance desired by the healthcare system. With these assurances, the system was willing to release funds earlier in the installation and product testing cycle in accordance with the vendor's desires.

In another case, a hospital negotiating team was not satisfied with the architectural services agreement proposed by their A/E firm because it contained a clause giving the architect ownership rights of all drawings and specifications prepared for the project. This clause was part of the standard form of contract recommended by the American Institute of Architects. The hospital executives were concerned that if something went wrong between the firm and the client during the design phase, they would be unable to take any work completed to date to another architectural firm for completion. The architect's position was that they wanted ownership rights so that the hospital could not take their design and sell it to other clients or reproduce the design at multiple sites. The problem was resolved by amending the contract to give the hospital title to all drawings and specifications and adding a clause stating that the design would not be sold by the hospital or replicated at any other sites other than the location specified in the agreement.

Reaching Agreement Through Bargaining

After you and the opponent have resolved all the issues you can through problem solving, you will have to attempt to reach agreement through the process of bargaining. Typically, the process of bargaining takes place when you have exhausted all other alternatives to resolving your differences. Bargaining requires both parties to make concessions. One party will make the first concession, usually followed by the other party making a concession. The process goes back and forth until a position is proposed that falls within the overlapping range of settlement that is accepted by both parties. Sometimes a concession you make on one issue is traded off by getting your opponent to make a concession on a different issue (commonly referred to as "horse trading"). Skill is required in knowing how and when to make concessions. As was mentioned earlier, obtaining early concession from the opponent is the most desirable. Similarly, delaying your concessions or making only small concessions in the early stages is another important bargaining step. Most skilled negotiators will never make two consecutive concessions without having received one from the opponent.

When you make a counteroffer, it should be one that you would find acceptable and that is within your range of settlement. In other words, your counteroffer should represent a reasonable settlement from your standpoint. The offer should be supportable—one that can be justified and withstand attack from the opponent. If you offer a concession with no reasonable support, the opponent will ask you, "How did you come up with your position?" If you cannot support this position, you will find yourself conceding further until you reach a point you can logically support, or you will continue to free-fall all the way to your opponent's position.

Be as conservative as possible when making concessions. Moving from your opening position all the way to the other end of your range of settlement on your first concession leaves you no room to maneuver if your opponent does not accept your counteroffer. Also, a large number of small concessions are desirable; you can then argue that your number of concessions demonstrate your reasonableness. Fabricating a concession pattern is an important prenegotiation step.

Skilled bargaining requires time. If you hurry the process along, the opponent will simply sit back and let you make one concession after another. Although this may be difficult if you are facing a deadline, if your opponent sees you starting to negotiate against yourself, he or she has little reason to make any further concession. The skilled negotiator will also exchange concessions on issues of secondary importance for those on issues of primary importance. Finally, the skilled negotiator will make concessions that essentially give nothing away. One way to do this is to concede on issues blown out of proportion or fabricated as "straw issues" during the initial presentation. When you make each counteroffer, make sure your opponent understands your position, your justification, and the benefits to them contained in your concession. Similarly, after your opponent makes a counteroffer, you might want to recess to examine the merits of the position, consider its importance to you, and prepare your next offer.

Even after bargaining to reach agreement on issues, some issues may still be left unresolved. At this time it may be best to cease further attempts to settle each unresolved issue individually. If possible, attempt to reach final agreement by looking at the outstanding issues and bargaining them as a total. If all the unresolved issues represent a small part of the entire transaction, bargaining for agreement as a total may bring a final resolution. For example, suppose you can agree on labor and overhead costs but cannot agree on material, administrative and general costs, and the profit rate in a supplier's proposal. As a final resort, try reaching agreement on total price rather than on each cost element. The bottom-line price is what you are concerned with most anyway.

During the bargaining phase, if both parties make offers and counteroffers, keep a careful written record of each one. Later in the negotiation, this list may become significant. For example, if you have made a larger number of concessions than your opponent, the list may be a basis to question the opponent's sincerity and desire to be reasonable. By counting concessions, you can see which party is making the most concessions and seek to rebalance in your favor.

PREPARING THE MEMORANDUM OF UNDERSTANDING

During the negotiations, each verbal agreement between the parties should be carefully recorded and signed off by each party. Particularly in complex negotiation situations with a large number of issues, parties will often either forget what has been agreed on or seek to retract agreements made during prior negotiating sessions. Moreover, verbal agreements often contain misunderstandings between the parties, and only after an agreement is placed in writing do the parties discover that no point of agreement has been reached.

After all the issues have been resolved, notes can then be translated into a written memorandum of understanding (MOU). If the opponent prepares the MOU, make sure to check it against your own notes from the negotiation to ensure that it represents your understanding and intent. The MOU should cover all areas of agreement, including references to intent where applicable. If the wording of the MOU is objectionable in any way, insist that it be rewritten to conform to your requirements and understanding.

Review and Approval of the Memorandum of Understanding

After the written MOU is completed to your satisfaction, it should be reviewed by all relevant parties at your organization before it is signed. This will ensure that the agreement reached is satisfactory to those affected by the transaction, your financial and legal experts, and your higher levels of authority. For example, on the purchase of a piece of radiology equipment, the MOU should be reviewed by the radiologists and the radiology department staff, biomechanical and engineering personnel, legal counsel, the CFO, and the CEO. If any member of your organization has objections to the MOU, you will need to take it up at another meeting with your opponent to attempt to resolve the issue.

The opponent should also sign the MOU only after it has been reviewed and approved by his or her institution. This will discourage any subsequent changes or second thoughts about the transaction. Considerable effort should be made in developing an accurate MOU with all information relevant to the intent and terms of the agreement. The MOU will frequently become the basis for a formal agreement between the two parties. If the MOU is to be turned over to legal counsel for the drafting of a written legal document, the need for accuracy in the MOU is further increased. With the approval of the final MOU or legal documentation, the negotiation process is completed.

CHAPTER 5

Optimizing the Negotiation Process

HAVE YOU EVER had a negotiation that just went the right way with seemingly little effort and tremendous results? A negotiation in which both parties seemed to understand the needs of one another and were willing to work toward those ends, where both sides recognized the contributions the opponent could make to the overall agreement, or where individuals were willing to set apart egos or the need for control? If you have experienced such a situation, you have recognized the power of an "optimized" negotiation. Although optimized negotiating situations are the exception rather than rule, a skillful negotiator will attempt to reach this higher level of negotiation whenever possible. In this chapter, the framework and philosophy of an optimized negotiation will be examined as well as the strategy it takes to move both the opponent and the negotiation process to this higher level.

INTEREST-BASED NEGOTIATING

Optimized negotiations are interest-based negotiations. In interest-based negotiating the objective is to reach an agreement that serves the best interests of all parties and leads to a mutually beneficial, long-term relationship. Although this process may not be applicable in a simple, one-time purchase of office supplies, it is apt to be beneficial in other situations, such as negotiating agreements between payers and providers or between providers themselves.

Interest-based negotiating requires a different attitude and focus from its participants during the basic process of the prenegotiation preparation and the formal negotiation phases. In the classroom, I often use an exercise to demonstrate this difference between traditional "transactional" negotiating attitudes versus the attitude of an interest-based negotiator. Classroom participants are asked to pair up with another person and assume an arm-wrestling position. Next, they are told that the objective of the exercise is to get the back of the other person's hand down on the table as many times as possible in 30 seconds. At the word "go," most participants will begin to struggle with each other in an attempt to move the other party's hand down to the table. With great effort and exertion, the stronger party will be able to get the opponent's hand down a few times in the time permitted. A few groups, however, will take a very different approach. They will simply begin going back and forth quickly, each allowing the other to get their hand down and both parties will score numerous times in the same amount of time. Following the laughter that usually concludes this exercise, we examine the different approaches that were taken by the two groups.

The first group concluded that in assuming an arm-wrestling position they were engaged in a contest in which they were to impose their own desires and seek to conquer the opponent. Similarly, when most people hear the word negotiation, they assume an arm-wrestling mindset in which they resist the efforts of the opponent and seek to impose their will in a unilateral fashion. This mindset requires great effort to persuade or otherwise force the opponent to capitulate. In such cases, the results are usually less than optimal. Many people adopt the arm-wrestling mindset when they are preparing to engage in a negotiation. They believe that their needs and desires are of paramount importance, while those of the opponent are secondary or nonexistent. They try to become as powerful as possible to "leverage" their opponent into accepting their position. By using superior strength and failing to consider the opponent's needs and desires, however, the relationship between the parties after the negotiation is usually strained at best.

The other groups, however, interpreted the stated objective of the exercise very differently. They heard that they were simply to get the other person's hand down as many times as possible. They did not interpret the exercise as a contest and therefore felt they could allow their hand to be put down as well. These groups viewed the exercise as a situation to be optimized through cooperation, and were able to get tremendous results for themselves and their opponent. In addition, the parties tended to view one another in a very favorable fashion following this experience and looked forward to working cooperatively again on future situations.

This simple exercise demonstrates the difference in attitudes and perspectives that exist in negotiations. One party (the arm wrestlers) viewed negotiating as an opportunity for a conquest, and the other party (interest-based optimizers) viewed negotiating as an opportunity to satisfy the interests of all parties in a cooperative and synergistic fashion. Why is interest-based negotiating an optimal way to reach agreement? First, as seen in the exercise, it typically yields tremendous results with very little effort on the part of the participants. Second, interest-based opponents will generally have better working relationships for the future. Finally, results of an interest-based negotiation are more likely to be a "gain-gain" agreement versus situations in which one party wins while the other party loses.

Win-Win Versus Gain-Gain

In almost any discussion of the negotiation process, the phrase "win-win" is mentioned. Although reaching a "win-win" agreement is noble, it may not be very realistic or achievable. To anyone who has ever played sports, the idea of both sides winning is hard to imagine.

Further, introducing a notion of "winning" tends to get parties thinking of a negotiation as a contest where the primary focus is on winning, at least initially. Using a gain-gain attitude, negotiators view the situation as an opportunity to create agreements that will benefit both parties. A gain-gain attitude allows for greater compromise from both sides as long as the end results are a net gain for each side. While the "win-win" approach to negotiation is a desirable goal, it has been my experience that win-win may not be possible and introduces a contest-like atmosphere to a negotiation. Having said that, I believe that Stephen Covey's idea of "win-win or walk away," from *The 7 Habits of Highly Effective People,* is certainly correct. He treats the subject with a more or less gain-gain approach.

ESTABLISHING AN ENVIRONMENT FOR INTEREST-BASED NEGOTIATING

Creating an environment where interest-based negotiating can take place is the first step for optimizing your negotiation. The skillful negotiator will seek to 1) assess and modify, if necessary, the views and attitudes of the participants approaching the bargaining table, and 2) use creativity in finding solutions and understanding the interdependencies involved in a complex healthcare situation.

Assessing and Modifying Views and Attitudes

When approaching the bargaining table, assess the participants' attitudes toward the negotiation. This "initial frame" is important because it will determine how the parties view both sides' positions, their willingness to cooperate, and how they will conduct the negotiations. In assessing the initial frame, consideration should be given to 1) properly defining the problem and the desired results, 2) the relationship between individuals and organizations, 3) having the right parties at the negotiating table, and 4) the negotiators' preferences and expectations of the negotiation process.

Defining the Problem and the Desired Results

Creating a proper "initial frame" requires that the parties ensure that the problems or issues are clearly understood. Although each party can define the problem or issue from his or her own perspective, usually the opponent sees a different problem or issue to be solved. Negotiating an agreement that does not adequately address unclear or unstated problems is very difficult. The agreements satisfy neither party's true interests. During the presentation of each parties' opening positions listen carefully and try to understand what each party seeks to achieve or resolve through the negotiated agreement.

For example, a group of physicians was negotiating with a health plan over a new provider contract. The physicians stated that their issues were related to patient access and quality of care issues; however, one unstated problem was their increasing overhead in complying with many of the medical management procedures instituted by the health plan. Considerable progress was achieved in resolving the physicians' stated issues, and yet the parties were unable to come to terms in an overall agreement. The physician's unstated issue of compensation for the increased overhead or, alternatively, reduction in the medical management demands was never addressed. Had the parties identified the issue of increasing the physician's reimbursement or modifying the management controls, a faster and more attractive resolution could have been reached.

In addition to defining problems and issues, some common ground for both parties needs to be articulated. In the arm-wrestling exercise where the two parties found common ground by allowing the other party to make gains, the opportunity to reach an optimized agreement was easily obtained. On the other hand, when the two parties saw no common ground and perceived the exercise as a contest, the results were different. Is there common ground between providers and payers? When this question is asked, the response is often, "of course, the patient." This response may be accurate in principle, but it fails to establish a more practical and common goal for both parties, that is, to increase business volumes. The health plan will be successful in increasing its number of enrollees if it is able to offer competitive premiums in the marketplace, which can be accomplished if providers are willing to accept a reasonable reimbursement for their services as well as control costs through diligent medical management. Although this agreement would have a short-term economic effect of reducing revenues for providers, by allowing the plan to build greater market share, the providers will see additional patient volumes which could make up for a reduced "revenues per unit of service" payment.

Relationships Between Individuals and Organizations

Whether a negotiation has an interest-based approach will also be determined by the relationship that exists between the parties at the table. Negotiating with a stranger is different than negotiating with a person with whom you are familiar and have established a good working relationship. When dealing with a stranger, a negotiator would probably be hesitant to offer the first concession quickly or expose too much about his or her position. The concern would be that the other party might use these actions as an opportunity to further press the opponent's desires and needs. On the other hand, when approaching the negotiating table with someone with whom you have successfully worked in the past and who has demonstrated sincerity and integrity, a negotiator will be much more willing to "lay the cards on the table."

The effects of this personal relationship were evident in a nationally acclaimed collaborative effort between two hospitals. The collaboration between the two institutions began when the CEO at one of the hospitals was replaced. Prior to the appointment of the new CEO, the two hospitals' chief executives had been engaged in a very competitive battle to dominate the service area through cannibalizing the other's markets, medical staff, patients, and employee base. The two CEOs viewed each other as competitors and their personal relationship was often strained. After the CEO at one of the hospitals was replaced, the incoming CEO met with the other hospital's chief executive. The two executives found they shared many common interests outside of healthcare, which led to the development of a strong friendship along with a sense of trust and cooperation. This camaraderie eventually led to discussions about how to best serve the community's healthcare needs and was the beginning of their collaborative efforts.

The relationship between healthcare organizations is also an important factor in the "initial frame." Since considerable rivalries between organizations have occurred over the years, many institutions carry around "baggage" from their skirmishes. This baggage creates an impediment when the parties seek a cooperative or collaborative atmosphere at the negotiating table. While conducting a board retreat several years ago for a large rural hospital system, I found that the trustees of two hospitals from adjacent communities were often at odds with one another. After questioning the people in the room about this matter, I discovered that the ill feelings went back to a high school football game that had been played between the two communities 30 years prior! Previously "adversarial" organizations are often required to sit down and negotiate some form of affiliation or merger in today's rapidly changing healthcare environment. When these parties carry their bad feelings to the negotiating table, battles may ensue as one party or the other seeks to correct past wrongs with a new agreement. Needless to say, many of these negotiations fall apart because neither party recognizes the benefits that might be achieved if they are able to put the past behind them.

Parties to the Negotiation

Far-reaching agreements that affect a multitude of parties are not unusual in healthcare today. For example, various employee groups, physician organizations, governmental agencies, and community groups all feel the effects of a merger between two medical centers. Making sure the interests of *all* parties are met is another important factor in interest-based negotiating.

Primary, secondary and tertiary parties. Three distinct parties in every negotiation each have their own respective needs and desires. Primary parties are the people who are physically present at the bargaining table. Secondary parties are the people directly affected by what is negotiated, and, finally, tertiary parties are people who will directly or indirectly feel the effects of whatever agreement is reached. To ensure that the right parties are present at the negotiating table, start with the interests of the tertiary parties. These parties may include the community, local employers, state regulatory agencies, and so forth. Their interests may be represented at the bargaining table by individuals from these groups or through a proxy such as a trustee representing the community's interests. Tertiary parties may also be represented by marketing personnel in the case of the local employers, or a consultant who understands the interests of state regulatory bodies.

Secondary parties typically want to have their own personal representative at the negotiating table as a primary party. When several medical groups are affected by a single provider agreement, each of the medical groups will want a member from their group present at the negotiating table. Similarly, in representing the entire medical staff, specialty physicians usually insist on one of their own at the negotiating table rather than a primary care physician (PCP). On the other hand, PCPs will usually insist on having a PCP at the table to look after their interests. In many of today's far-reaching healthcare negotiations, numerous secondary parties may require representation at the negotiating table. If the number at the table is too large, negotiating will be difficult, if not impossible. In these situations, conduct a "consensus building" negotiation among the secondary parties prior to the actual negotiation. During this initial negotiation, preapproved goals and ranges of settlement will be agreed to so that the group can then be represented by a smaller number of primary parties at the actual negotiation.

Negotiation Process Expectations

Understanding the process of negotiation that the opponent intends to follow is another important step in trying to reach an optimized situation. If the opponent sees negotiation as an opportunity for conquest (i.e., the arm-wrestling scenario), interest-based bargaining will be difficult. The negotiator might attempt to reorient the opponent's perspective of the process by explaining the difference between the traditional arm-wrestling approach and an interest-based approach with a promise of greater benefits and less effort. While some opponents may be receptive to this way of thinking, some people will not change their way of thinking or style of negotiating. A negotiator must be prepared for this and modify his or her approach where necessary. This "lowest common denominator of negotiation" is a reality that must be understood and accepted. Unfortunately, interest-based negotiating only takes place where the parties are willing and have the requisite knowledge to bargain at this level.

Introducing Creativity into the Negotiation

Interest-based negotiators tend to be creative people. They recognize that the healthcare landscape is continually changing and look at creative opportunities to address marketplace dynamics. Seldom in optimized negotiations will you hear the words, "that is the way we have always done it here." You will find an innovative atmosphere that reflects the thinking of "why not?" rather than "why should we?"

Creative problem solving is often introduced during these negotiations. Through brainstorming or other creative techniques, participants can propose possible solutions to the identified problems. Process improvement techniques such as cause and effect diagramming and variance analysis are often tools used to break down problems into root causes that can lead to innovative solutions. Healthcare executives have many different ideas about what future healthcare systems in this country will look like. One common theme, however, is that it will look nothing like it does today. Parties who are willing to introduce innovative solutions at the negotiating table and to adapt to the changing healthcare environment will succeed.

Understanding Interdependencies when Negotiating Agreements

Negotiators need to consider the effects of their agreements on the parties to the agreement. Healthcare is a complex business in which numerous cause and effect relationships exist; a good agreement must reflect "whole systems thinking." A good agreement is not suboptimized for any particular party but rather considers how it will affect all entities within the agreement's influence. For example, a hospital is a collection of many departments that need to function effectively if the overall organization is to succeed. An agreement that provides favorable treatment, such as an excessive budget, for any department may imperil the overall health of the hospital.

Today's healthcare landscape is populated with great providers, health plans, suppliers, and other entities. Each of these parts, however, constitutes a single component in the overall healthcare industry. Each component is essential for the industry to succeed. Without providers, there can be no provision of services; without health plans there would be no financing mechanism; and without suppliers the tools necessary to provide care would not exist. Each component, therefore, is interdependent. The key to creating the most efficient overall healthcare system will involve recognizing these interdependencies and negotiating agreements that take into account the cause and effect relationship between the components.

Unfortunately, interdependent relationships are often at odds with many people's independent nature. Many people are raised to become independent and this approach to living carries over into professional lives and can even be reflected in the occupations we choose. Many physicians, for instance, chose to enter their field because of the freedom to be their own boss. Even in the establishment of an independent physician association (IPA), the nature of the entity is to be an independent physician organization. This desire for independence is often reflected at the negotiating table where one party expresses the attitude that "you need us, but we do not need you." While this may be true in some cases, recognizing that there are fundamental interdependencies among parties to any agreement is important in creating an optimized agreement. Additionally, by recognizing these interdependencies, parties may find new ways to coordinate their efforts in a manner that maximizes the gains for all.

THE COURTSHIP NEGOTIATION PROCESS

Interest-based negotiating is intended to lead to mutually beneficial, long-term relationships serving the interests of both parties. The analogy of a personal relationship can be helpful in understanding the process by which negotiators can reach this result. In courting and ultimately marrying a spouse, the process of interest-based negotiation is typically followed. If done correctly, both parties are hoping to develop a long-term, mutually beneficial marriage. Anyone who has been through this courting process understands, possibly only subconsciously, the steps of the interest-based negotiator as the process proceeds from initially developing a personal relationship to negotiating an initial agreement (i.e., getting to the altar).

Building the Initial Relationship

At the outset of the courting process, a person begins dating the person he or she will eventually marry. The two may be initially attracted for reasons such as physical attractiveness, common hobbies, or mutual interests. Similarly, in the world of healthcare, two parties are attracted to one another because of perceived complementary benefits, mutual needs, or recognition of interdependency.

At this stage, each person starts to gain an understanding of the other person's interests, needs, desires, and so forth. On the first few dates, the questions are probably not too serious nor is either willing to "bare their soul" yet. The same can be said for the initial stages of the interest-based negotiation process. If a negotiator is not familiar with the opponent, he or she may want to get a sense of the opponent's business culture and philosophy, strategic direction, or business model. Additionally, it may be helpful to develop a better relationship with your opponent on a personal basis. The parties can develop a sense of trust and integrity that will allow both to feel comfortable further exposing positions as the process continues. In some cultures, negotiation parties may spend a considerable amount of time talking about anything but the deal at hand. During these times the parties begin to feel comfortable with one another and become ready to move to the next step in the process.

Expressing Issues and Concerns

Once the dating phase had progressed to a point where both people have developed a sense of trust and basic compatibility, the next step is to look at compatibility on major issues or concerns. During courtship, these discussions might include issues such as children, religion, and lifestyle choices. Such discussions must be entered with some trepidation. If, for instance, the two discover that they have vastly different opinions on these issues, any future relationship would certainly be in peril. These issues are not generally discussed with a total stranger or on the first date; however, they are matters that help two people form a basic agreement.

When two parties are negotiating a business agreement, similar discussions should take place to uncover any fundamental incompatibilities that would prevent a long-term, mutually beneficial relationship. For example, a health plan and a provider group were negotiating a joint venture for a new preferred provider organization (PPO) when they discovered that their ultimate goals were not the same. The health plan wanted to introduce the PPO as a short term, limited-scope demonstration project, while the provider group wanted the PPO to be a long-term project that would grow significantly and capture a significant percentage of the local market. Had this incompatibility not been discovered early in their discussions, significant disagreements later in the relationship would have been inevitable. Eventually, the relationship would fail as one party or the other felt that its interests were not being met by the agreement. Another situation occurred when two hospitals that were conducting merger discussions looked at the issue of clinical integration. Their talks revealed that one organization was in favor of integrating clinical departments to reduce redundancies and lower costs, while the potential partner thought that each institution should maintain autonomy of clinical programs and use the merger simply to get broader geographical coverage. Needless to say, the merger discussions were terminated.

Developing Mutual Objectives

After reaching agreement on major issues or concerns, the courtship process turns to developing mutual objectives. The next step in the courtship will involve a "dreaming of our life together" discussion. At this exciting point in the process, the two start proposing how they anticipate a life together. They discuss issues such as raising children, where to live, and lifestyle. These agreed-on objectives are based on both parties' interests, needs, and desires. In a business negotiation, the discussion will revolve around the desired results of the potential agreement in terms of profitability, quality improvement, market share growth, and other factors. This is an important step in the "courtship" for two reasons. First, it produces specific objectives both parties have agreed should be the focus of the agreement, and it can serve as a basis for determining later on whether the agreement is working. Second, by developing mutual objectives, both parties create the enthusiasm that will help them proceed toward a beneficial agreement. This can later develop into a more conciliatory approach as the negotiation continues.

Creating Opportunities for Mutual Gain

Once the objectives of the agreement have been determined, the parties need to look at how those objectives can be accomplished. The parties should look at the respective strengths and weaknesses of each partner and develop a plan that maximizes the effectiveness of the agreement. In the marriage analogy, this may have taken place as a "division of labor" discussion. If one person is financially oriented, the role of managing the family finances may be delegated to that person. Similarly, agreements will be made as to who will be primarily responsible for cooking, home repairs, child rearing, or social planning. Two business entities might discuss similar matters as they look at drafting the optimal agreement. If one has marketing expertise, it may take that role while the other might assume responsibility for matters such as billings and collections. The issue of control must be set aside and the focus should be on what combination of roles and responsibilities creates the greatest synergy in the agreement.

Developing the Initial Agreement

At the end of the courtship, an initial agreement will be developed between the parties. With a couple, this might take place in a church as they pledge their commitment to one another. For business entities, this step is usually completed with the drafting of the legal documents outlining the negotiated agreement. This is simply an initial agreement in the relationship. Although the two parties have made considerable efforts in establishing a sound and well thought-out agreement, modifications will likely be necessary in the future. Consider the prenuptial commitments made between a couple; the couple will likely renegotiate several details related to their agreement during the first year or two of marriage. If, however, the basic issues and concerns were agreed to during the courtship process, these renegotiations are typically over minor details that are easily worked out. If major issues or concerns were not addressed early in the courtship process, then the resulting problems might threaten the long-term relationship. Similarly in healthcare, problems result from the changing marketplace, new competitors, and the changing needs of the parties after the initial agreement has been reached. Fortunately, as long as the initial values and concerns have not changed, adjustment to the agreement is usually possible. In interest-based negotiations, the relationship both parties leave the bargaining table with is often more important than any particular outcome.

Components of a Successful Agreement

The agreeement arrived at at the end of the courtship serves as the framework for the relationship moving forward. This agreement must reflect the objectives agreed to, the methods by which those objectives will be reached, how the success of the agreement will be measured, and how each party will be held accountable and compensated for their participation. Five basic elements should be included in every agreement reached through interest-based bargaining: the desired results, guidelines, resources, accountability, and consequences of the agreement. The ability to align these elements is critical if the agreement is to be implemented without undue difficulty—"a good agreement is one that never needs to be referred to."

1. Desired results. Specific desired results and objectives must be identified in a good agreement. The desired results should have been discussed in general during the courtship, when the parties were developing mutual objectives, and should be further detailed during this step. The desired results may be stated in terms of market share percentages, utilization rates, or performance specifications. When possible, desired results should be stated as specifically as possible. An agreement to simply launch a new joint venture may prove problematic later if one party or the other wishes to challenge the success or failure of the venture. If, on the other hand, specific targets or goals have been stated up front and those goals are met, the issue can be easily resolved. In some cases, however, it may not be possible to be so specific. When two institutions merge, for example, a shared vision may be the desired result with no further details possible.

Sometimes one party may be reluctant to state specific desired results. Getting a physician to state that making money is a primary objective for a provider contract, or getting an employee to identify their executive aspirations, is often a difficult task. Failing to make these objectives explicit in the agreement, however, will make achieving an agreement aimed at accomplishing these goals difficult.

2. Guidelines. Guidelines need to be established about how the parties will participate in the agreement. These guidelines may delineate roles of the participants, the policies on which the participants will act, or mechanisms for decision making. Often, the terms and conditions of an agreement are simply spelling out the rules by which the participants will function within the agreement.

3. Resources. Identifying resource requirements is another important element in negotiating a good agreement. Estimating what resources are required and who will provide those resources is essential. While financial resources are usually addressed, other "soft" resources must be given attention, resources such as information or data, human resources, and access to existing customers.

4. Performance measurement and accountability. Systems to measure the performance of the agreement must also be put into place. After the desired results have been identified, the means to measure their accomplishment must be established along with a schedule for when the measurements will take place. The accomplishment of departmental goals within a specified timeline is one example that might be used in an employment agreement with a department head. Tied in with measuring performance is the factor of accountability. Parties to the agreement need to be held accountable for accomplishing the desired results in the agreement for which they are responsible. Those responsible for the marketing function might be held accountable for market share targets while those providing healthcare services should be measured against utilization rate or cost per enrollee targets.

5. Consequences. Most good agreements will contain risk and reward provisions related to the performance of each party under the terms of the agreement. Both risk and reward should be part of the agreement to provide incentives for exemplary performance and penalties for not meeting expectations.

In developing the initial agreement, all five of these elements must be adequately addressed and aligned. Difficulties encountered during the implementation of an agreement can often be traced back to the omission of one or more of these elements or the misalignment of one element in relation to the others. Which of these elements are commonly addressed and which are often left out? In negotiating agreements, most parties will focus their efforts on discussing issues of guidelines and resources. These elements are the easiest to identify and negotiate. Issues of accountability and consequences are also usually dealt with but are occasionally omitted or misaligned. Under discounted fee-for-service contracts, a physician is often measured by his or her ability to decrease utilization of services but is seldom rewarded with any share of the cost savings.

This misalignment results in a decreased incentive for the physician to manage care, which is typically one of the desired results of the agreement. *In most situations, however, failing to clearly identify the desired results causes poor or misaligned agreement.* Desired results are sometimes difficult to identify and can also lead to the uncomfortable issues of accountability and risk. As discussed above, some parties may be reluctant to identify specific results. Sometimes, it may also be embarrassing for a party to admit to desired results involving personal income, prestige, more recognition, need for economic security, and so forth.

The four elements of guidelines, resources, accountability, and consequences need to be structured and aligned in a way to accomplish the first element—desired results. Agreements that are vague or that are subject to disputes during their implementation often fail to target desired results or specific outcomes. I once heard a skilled negotiator say, "every agreement is perfectly aligned to get the results it gets." If the results or targets are not clear, the rest of the agreement will suffer a similar malady.

TIPS FOR KEEPING NEGOTIATIONS ON THE HIGH ROAD

Optimizing the negotiating process can occur with interest-based negotiating along with a sound initial frame. During the actual negotiations, however, it can be a challenge to continually keep the discussions on this "high road." While negotiations often begin with an emphasis on mutual interest and a stated desired to consummate an agreement that will be beneficial to all parties, commonly the negotiation can degrade into one of positional bargaining or simple "haggling." Unfortunately, once a negotiation takes off in the direction of the "low road," bringing it back to a higher level may be difficult, if not impossible.

To maintain a more productive negotiation, the following are some ideas for strengthening an interest-based environment:

- create motivators for changing positions;
- be prepared to give;
- introduce creative solutions;
- satisfy desires, not stated demands;
- substantiate expectations and remove fantasies;
- put principles aside; and
- keep control issues off the table.

Create Motivators for Changing Positions

Changing the opponent's position on issues is at the core of any negotiation. Persuasive arguments and the use of logic, threats, or deadlines are some of the techniques that can be used to overcome a party's natural reluctance to change. However, in overcoming this reluctance, a negotiator can either move the negotiation in a positive direction or create a more adversarial environment. Use of threats such as, "you need to change your position on this issue or we will cancel our current agreement" does little to create a sense of "courtship" and will often result in the use of threats by the opponent in retaliation. In optimized negotiations, changes in the opponent's position are better accomplished by creating the motivation for the opponent. By suggesting that a provider may want to accept a lower inpatient per diem, the health plan can hold out the prospect of both greater volumes and additional use of outpatient services. With the promise of increased revenues elsewhere, a strong motivation exists to concede the inpatient rate.

Be Prepared to Give

As an old saying in negotiation goes, "If you want to get, you have to be prepared to give." Little interest-based negotiating will take place when a party is simply interested in collecting as many concessions from the opponent as possible while yielding as few as possible. This is not to say one should try to optimize a negotiation by making a large number of significant concessions, but rather that negotiation is a give-and-take process. What is conceded, and when it is conceded, can be significant in trying to create an optimized negotiation.

In the arm-wrestling exercise, think about what your reaction would be if your opponent's first move were to exert considerable pressure trying to force your hand down. Your immediate response would probably be to resist this pressure and apply an equal or greater pressure toward your opponent. If on the other hand, your opponent were willing to yield to you first, it probably would lead to your willingness to allow them the next win. Similarly, in negotiation if the first statement by either party is, "we want this" or "we need that" the other party's immediate response is to question what is in it for them. As an alternative, a party might suggest that, "we see the merits of your position on the issue and we think we can get there, if you can consider our need to achieve a concession on this other issue." By demonstrating the willingness to give first, your opponent may be more willing to consider your needs and interests somewhere else.

Introduce Imagination and Creative Solutions

If you think over your own negotiation experiences, you may recognize that some of your "best" agreements have involved innovative or creative new solutions. Simply refining your party's present positions or trying to keep to "business as usual" seldom leads to an optimized agreement. By introducing imagination and creativity into the negotiation process, the likelihood of finding better solutions that serve the interest of all parties is enhanced. If someone had suggested 25 years ago that health plans and providers should integrate the financing and delivery of healthcare, an eyebrow or two would have been raised. Today, the industry has numerous examples where providers and payers have done just that. This has resulted in opening the door to true "managed care" and developed concepts such as risk sharing, data mining, and chronic disease management.

In optimized negotiations, the phrase, "but that's not the way we have always done it here" is seldom heard. Useful creativity tools such as brainstorming can often be used at the negotiating table to find new creative ideas or solutions. Although many of the ideas may be too "far out" to represent a practical solution, the suggestion that these ideas lie at the far end of the range of settlement may also serve as a means to begin moving the opponent off his or her own tried-and-true position.

Satisfy Desires, Not Stated Demands

In presenting their respective positions, both parties in a negotiation have expressed their stated demands. It is important, however, to look behind the stated demands to find out what the opponent's true desires may be. Similar to mutual problem-solving techniques discussed earlier, an opportunity exists to satisfy the opponent's desires in other ways than by simply acquiescing to his or her stated demands. A physician seeking an employment contract may have a stated demand for an extremely high salary level that is above market rates or the amount budgeted. Through questioning, it may become apparent that the physician's true desire may be to enjoy a comfortable lifestyle today while also providing for adequate retirement income. In such a case, it may be possible to satisfy these desires by negotiating a lower salary level with an increased amount of deferred compensation or retirement benefits.

Another classic example in healthcare is the *stated demands* by most health plans that 100 percent of their physician network adhere to stringent and, to most physicians, intrusive utilization management controls. The *desired goal* of the health plan is to avoid inappropriate or unnecessary utilization of services. When questioned about the need to monitor 100 percent of the physician community for excess utilization, health plans willingly agree that only 25 to 40 percent of the physicians need to be monitored. They recognize little benefit from monitoring the remaining 60 to 75 percent; in fact, such monitoring only increases their costs for additional staffing in their utilization management departments. In one such case, physicians negotiating with a health plan were able to get an agreement whereby those physicians who were in the top 50 percent in terms of being efficient utilizers would no longer be required to call for reauthorizations, second opinions, and so forth. Not only was the desire of the health plan met, but it was able to lower its utilization management costs at the same time. Efficient physicians in their network were also pleased with the solution, as they no longer were required to spend valuable time complying with the unnecessary demands for utilization controls. A further benefit of the agreement was that physicians who were subject to utilization controls began to change their practice patterns to be free of the utilization controls. The final effect was improved utilization by all providers in the network resulting in substantial savings to the health plan.

One way to find out the opponent's true desire is simply to ask questions. By asking why the opponent desires a particular concession or what problems he or she has with the position presented, the opponent's *true* desires may be discovered. It has been suggested that by simply asking "why" five times, the real issue will be discovered.

Substantiate Expectations and Remove Fantasies

Unrealistic expectations present a significant challenge for conducting optimized negotiations. An opponent may adopt such a position, however, based on a failure to consider the impact of his or her position in terms of the other party's interests or needs, because he or she has been given erroneous information, or simply by adopting an arbitrary or emotional position. Expectations must be supportable and substantiated before continuing the negotiation process. Failure to create such expectations may result in unrealistic expectations that will be difficult to change later in the negotiation.

During the prenegotiation preparation phase, a good negotiator will have established a range of settlement for the opponent. At one end of the range is the opponent's highest level of expectation. If the opponent's actual expectations are above this level, and are unrealistic, a negotiator needs to quickly move the opponent out of this fantasy world. Always ask the opponent to support the expectation. If the opponent does not have a supportable position, a negotiator has to move the opponent from this position. It may be advisable to educate the opponent on what the range of settlement might be. Comparable data, similar agreements, or industry averages are good logical arguments to use in such situations.

Sometimes, it is better not to attempt to change the opponent's expectations but rather advise him or her of the consequences of the stated position. A "choices and consequences" approach may help the opponent be more realistic. This technique is often used in the "tiered network" strategy employed by many health plans. In essence, the health plan proposes a suggested rate schedule to providers. Providers are free to accept the rates and be placed in a "preferred" network, or, alternatively, they can choose to be reimbursed at a higher level and be placed in a "not-so-preferred" network. When designing the plan's benefits, the health plan structures the deductible and copayment schedules to give attractive benefits to members choosing to use the preferred network. By making the *choice* for higher reimbursement, the "not-so-preferred" providers suffer the *consequence* of much lower patient volumes.

Put Principles Aside (Sometimes)

Personal or organizational principles are important guidelines in judging the adequacy of an agreement. A good negotiator will have difficulty accepting an agreement where their principles are either not addressed or violated. Although principles such as ethics and moral values should not be compromised, some principles can get in the way of reaching an agreement. For example, a completed hospital building project was discovered to have a serious problem with the ventilation system. It was unclear who was responsible for the problem; evidence pointed to several parties including the architect, the general contractor, and the mechanical subcontractor. The corrective solution for the problem involved modifications costs of around $70,000. The architect firmly believed he was not at fault for the problem, and, based on his principles, he felt he should not be responsible for any payment to correct the solution. Similarly, both the general contractor and the mechanical subcontractor were unwilling to pay for the repairs. In the end, the owner of the building took all three parties to arbitration. Legal fees for each of the three defendants were in excess of $50,000. In addition, the arbitrator assessed each party one-third of the responsibility for paying to fix the ventilation system. Most damaging to the three parties, however, was that the owner then refused to consider any of the parties for further projects. As a famous litigation attorney once said, "My clients can have just as much principle as they can afford. Usually when the legal fees reach around $100,000, they decide the principle isn't that important."

Keep "Control" Issues Off the Table

In the world of healthcare agreements, control can often be a significant issue. While control obsessiveness may not be the norm, it is certainly in ample supply. In negotiations, the battle over control can cause great conflict, consume far too much effort, and result in very little ultimate value. Control issues may be raised over significant matters such as management of the organization or control of the financial resources, or it may concern lesser issues such as control over the drafting of the legal documents. One wise healthcare system CEO once said, "It is much smarter to make sure that the system is in control rather than attempting to control the system." In negotiating an agreement, it is more important to have an aligned agreement that will achieve its desired objectives than it is to negotiate the control over the participants to the agreement. Typically, issues of control are as much emotional as they are logical. When the issue of control is related to a person's ego or insecurities, a negotiator must find other ways to address the desires or needs of the opponent. Recognition in the form of job titles or awards may be one ego-boosting technique. Laying out a succession plan for a high-level executive may mitigate feelings of insecurity and lessen the need for control.

REFERENCE

Covey, S. R. 1989. *The 7 Habits of Highly Effective People*. New York: Fireside.

CHAPTER 6

Negotiating Techniques

SKILLED NEGOTIATORS MAKE frequent use of numerous negotiating techniques. While some may be more effective than others, be aware of the techniques available to you as well as the techniques your opponent may employ. Get acquainted with these techniques and be prepared to use them in situations where their use will improve or enhance your negotiating position or outcome. The following describes many of the most commonly used techniques.

EMPHASIZING MUTUAL INTEREST

Throughout the negotiation, remind the opponent that the objective is to reach a mutually beneficial agreement. Emphasizing mutual interest can alleviate the opponent's fears that his or her interests will go unmet. At the same time, however, remind the opponent that he or she will not always get everything, that both parties must consider each other's interests, and that concessions must be made to consummate a mutually beneficial agreement. Emphasizing the need to work out the best arrangement for both parties will also add a positive tone to the negotiation session and keep discussions moving along in a productive direction.

This technique may be helpful in dealing with physicians who might otherwise overlook the interests of the hospital, other physicians, their patients, or the community. It may also be helpful in dealing with a health plan that might otherwise ignore the needs for adequate reimbursement to providers to maintain a strong provider network required to sell the health plan product. The starting point in many negotiations should be to establish mutual interests and translate those interests into mutual objectives for the agreement. While the parties may feel that their interests are well-known or self-evident, review both parties' interests and ask questions to clarify your understanding of those interests as well as to identify any additional interests that may exist.

USE OF QUESTIONS

Asking questions is an excellent negotiating tool for two major reasons. First, questions help uncover information from the opponent or can clarify the opponent's positions, sense of reality, and priorities. Second, asking questions assists a negotiator in controlling the tone and flow of the negotiation. Questions may also be used to stimulate thoughts in the mind of the opponent, to get his response to alternatives you might be proposing, to push the opponent into making a decision, or to obtain information regarding his viewpoint about your positions or interests.

Examples of questions that obtain information:

1. Could you show me how you got to that figure?
2. Will you explain that point to me?
3. What objections do you have to our proposal?

Examples of questions that stimulate thought:

1. Would you consider a joint venture opportunity in this situation?
2. Are you sure?
3. Have you thought about expanding your range of services, Doctor Smith?

Examples of questions that can cause decisions to be made:

1. Are you prepared to give us a contract if we reduce our prices by 10 percent?
2. Did you know the price is going up beginning next month?
3. Which do you prefer, a long-term or a short-term contract?

Examples of questions that give information:

1. Have you had a chance to look at our new proposal? Let me show you how we have tried to accommodate your interests.
2. If I understand you correctly, you are afraid our reimbursement rate is too low, aren't you?
3. We recently completed a patient satisfaction survey. Do you know what we've found?

Information is bargaining power, and asking questions allows the negotiator to gather information to increase bargaining power. When you are answering your opponent's questions, you are giving away information and may be losing bargaining power. You may have experienced the desperate feeling in a negotiation when you are on the defensive and answering numerous questions. Some negotiators, however, fail to make use of this very effective negotiating technique. Some of the reasons for not asking questions are:

1. Fear that asking questions might reveal ignorance.
2. Fear of showing that questioner has not been paying attention.

3. Questions that come to mind are forgotten in the heat of the negotiation.
4. Fear of embarrassing the other party.
5. A preference for talking rather than listening; questions are designed for listening, not talking.
6. Lack of persistence and follow-up on poorly answered questions.

If any or all of these reasons have affected your willingness to use questions in the past, you must seek to overcome your resistance in this area. Many types of questions can be asked during a negotiation, including general questions, specific questions, leading questions, suggestive questions, or successive questions.

General Questions

General questions are useful in probing for new facts or information. The best time to use these questions is during the early stages of the negotiation when the parties are still trying to verify each other's views of reality, positions, and supporting information. Generally, the opponent will answer most, if not all, of your general questions without suspicion. Some examples of general questions are:

1. I know you have a contract with our competitor, Acme Health Plan. What do you think of them?
2. What is your experience in the marketing of healthcare services for the elderly? How long have you been doing this?

Asking general questions later in a negotiation runs the risk of reopening issues that may have already been agreed on. Also, if you keep asking general questions after specific terms have been put on the table, the opponent may wonder if you are really prepared or knowledgeable about the subject at hand.

Specific Questions

Specific questions call for fairly confined answers. While they may be best used in the later stages of a negotiation, you can also raise them early in the process. In the later part of a negotiation, however, you will be more apt to know exactly what you are after when you ask a specific question. Some examples of specific questions are:

1. Is this facility fully zoned for use as a medical office building?
2. Can you describe the conditions that caused you to cancel our current provider agreement?

Try to be a specific as possible in your questions. The more precise your questions, the better chance you have of getting a precise answer.

Leading Questions

Leading questions are typically statements that have been turned into questions. A leading question always calls for a "yes" answer. When asking a leading question, you already know what the opponent's response will be. It is simply a means to get an admission on a specific point. Examples of leading questions are:

1. This is a very profitable company, isn't it?
2. I have done an excellent job and really deserve a raise, don't I?

The main problem in asking leading questions is that you must be confident about the answer. If you ask a leading question and it is answered negatively, you will need to reassert your position with further arguments.

Suggestive Questions

Suggestive questions are intended to result in a specific course of action or suggestion. The object of suggestive questions is to have the opponent either commit to a course of action or explain why he or she is unwilling to do so. When trying to explain away your suggestion, the opponent will be on the defensive and will have to present strong logical arguments for the rejection. Suggestive questions might include:

1. Don't you think it's better to sign the contract now?
2. Isn't this the best time to seize a market opportunity and invest in this joint venture?

Suggestive questions appear far less aggressive than leading questions. Therefore, try to use suggestive questions in obtaining a specific course of action or decision whenever possible.

Successive Questions

Successive questions are used to maintain control and develop positive bargaining momentum in the negotiations. This questioning technique uses a series of questions that will build up to a final question reflecting your ultimate objective. The questions continually build your case until the total sum of your questions achieves the outcome you desire. An example of successive questions leading up to your request for a 10-percent increase in reimbursement from a health plan might be:

1. Why shouldn't we receive a rate increase?
2. Haven't we been a solid part of your provider network?
3. Haven't we coordinated our services with your medical management staff?

4. Doesn't our utilization data show we have reduced costs by over 10 percent?
5. Haven't you been able to achieve premium increases in the marketplace?
6. Based on all these facts, don't you think it's fair and reasonable to give us a 10-percent increase in our reimbursement rates across the board?

The object of using successive questions is to make your case without being interrupted. Be cautious when using this technique so as not to annoy or intimidate the opponent.

Answering the Opponent's Questions

Knowing when and how to answer questions is also important in negotiating. When the opponent asks a question that you feel is appropriate, you should not hesitate to answer. A refusal may cause the opponent to become suspicious of your motives or reduce the level of trust between the two parties. Refusing to answer questions also makes you appear less cooperative and may cause an equal and opposite reaction in your opponent. This "playing your cards close to your vest" environment is a major obstacle to creating an optimized negotiation situation.

At other times, however, you will encounter questions that you should not or do not want to answer. Some approaches to avoid answering questions without offending the opponent might be:

1. Claim ignorance—Simply say that you do not know the answer. You may appear unprepared or uninformed, however, and may be required to seek out the information before the negotiation can proceed.
2. Claim irrelevance—State, "I'm not sure that question pertains to the issue we are discussing," or "I don't

understand your purpose in asking that question." If your response is mild, it should not upset the opponent. Moreover, the opponent will likely choose not to follow up with another question.

3. Refuse to answer—Suggest that the question requires information you would rather not disclose at this time. You might suggest that you would be willing to share this information later in the negotiation process if progress on other issues has been made.

4. Respond with your own questions—Answering the opponent's question with a question of your own is often a good way to avoid the question and regain control of bargaining momentum. This must be done tactfully so that you do not appear stubborn or obnoxious to your opponent.

PATIENCE AND THE PACE OF NEGOTIATIONS

Patience is one of the most powerful tactics in negotiation. Using patience, persistence, and determination, the skillful negotiator can make up for inadequate resources or bargaining power. Patience may allow the negotiator to divide the opponent's negotiating team or organization, lower expectations, achieve multiple concessions without making one, force the opponent to reconsider priorities, or separate wishes from reality. Patience may also raise new problems or issues to the surface, get other people involved, or cause a change in the leadership of the opponent's team. On the other hand, slowing down the negotiations could increase expenses for one or both sides, force the opponent to look elsewhere for an agreement, or result in a deadlock or walkout. Finally, slowing the process can be tiring, take you away from other work, and increase levels of stress in all parties.

Patience proved to be an effective attack in the recent acquisition of a medical office building owned by several physicians. The medical center that was interested in acquiring the office building made an initial offer to the physician group that was subsequently rejected by the group. The physicians then proposed a counteroffer to the medical center. Rather than responding quickly, the medical center's negotiating team chose to stay quiet and be patient. Over a period of three weeks, several of the physicians began to look again at the medical center's opening offer since they had no other potential buyers for the property. This "splinter" group of physicians, who were possibly motivated by needs to liquidate their assets or the simple fact that they had not received any other offers, began to express their desire to reconsider the medical center's offer. Eventually, a majority of the physicians came to view the medical center's offer as acceptable and the deal was completed. The final agreement was close to the level where the medical center had started with a few minor concessions to alleviate hard feelings among a few "hold out" physicians.

An important lesson from this example is that a negotiating team's unified position will typically erode over time. A negotiator can often achieve an objective simply by "waiting out" the opponent's team. This is commonly seen in union negotiations once a strike has been called. As the strike continues, many union members began to view a prolonged strike as unacceptable and are increasingly willing to agree to less favorable terms to end the strike.

More simply put, almost all negotiators will naturally move through their range of settlement over time if they desire an agreement. By remaining patient, you allow the opponent to continue moving toward your position until an acceptable point is reached. Sometimes an impatient negotiator may "negotiate against himself" by making several consecutive concessions until he or she reaches a point where the opponent is willing to agree.

Being patient also allows the negotiator to fulfill the basic objective of interest-based negotiating. It gives a negotiator the opportunity to get a perspective on the situation before resolving specific issues. Understanding the issues, assessing risks, testing the opponent's strengths and weaknesses, and understanding the opponent's priorities and expectations usually take time. Patience gives the negotiator an opportunity to understand all of these factors prior to initiating the actual bargaining of issues. Additionally, patience will give the opponent and his or her organization time to understand your positions, interests, and priorities. In a rushed negotiation, many of these factors are never discovered or discussed.

Another benefit of patience is that it allows the negotiator a chance to find out how best to benefit each party. Before the negotiation begins, neither party can know the best way to resolve the problems, issues, or risks. As new information is brought to light, new alternatives may be discovered. Patient bargaining usually results in benefits to both sides. Unfortunately, many negotiators seem to want to rush the negotiation process either to meet a deadline or to fulfill a desire to get things done. Many negotiators engage in the process as if they were playing tennis. One party will serve up an opening offer. The other side will quickly make a counteroffer, and back and forth they will go until a quick resolution is reached.

Culturally, Americans are impatient negotiators, whereas other cultures are much more patient. A good example was the negotiation to end the Vietnam War through the Paris peace accords. The North Vietnamese contingent went to Paris and rented a villa for two years. The American negotiating team rented a villa for two weeks. When the negotiations began, the two parties spent almost six months simply agreeing on the shape of the negotiating table and the parties that would be present. Anyone who has ever negotiated with a Japanese company knows the pace of their negotiations is much slower than those we experience in the United States. Even within the United States, the pace of healthcare negotiations seems to be much faster in the Northeast and the Western states. As you reach the Midwest and the South, things slow down considerably at the negotiating table.

While patience is an enviable characteristic for any negotiator, it does not come naturally to many healthcare executives. "Type A" personalities typify the industry. If you are one of these individuals, you must convince yourself that your outcome will be driven to a large extent by your ability to think and act patiently. Another reason to slow down is to remember that any time saved by rushing during the negotiation will probably be spent tenfold trying to implement a poorly reasoned agreement. This is not to say that negotiations should be conducted at a snail's pace. The need to meet deadlines, or to simply get work done, dictates that some level of speed is required in every negotiation. However, you always want to move *relatively slower* than the opponent. If the opponent is trying to negotiate at 55 miles an hour, you will want to go 50. If, on the other hand, your opponent is willing to proceed at 90 miles an hour, you can speed up to 85. The secret is having the opponent moving faster than you.

The pace of a negotiation can be orchestrated to a certain extent. In some situations speeding up the proceedings is to your advantage; at other times it will be in your best interest to slow things down. A careful analysis of which side is feeling pressure to reach an agreement will help determine the pace of negotiations. Generally, if the pressure is on the opponent, you want to prolong the negotiation and slow things down. If the pressure is on you, however, it may be preferable to quicken the pace to move the negotiation forward.

In a typical buyer-seller situation, the pressure is usually on the seller. The seller may be feeling pressure because of sales quotas or competition and will typically start pushing hard for a conclusion or decision. In such situations, the buyer will want to take it slowly. Time is on the buyer's side. In slowing things down and possibly walking away temporarily, the buyer will find the deal rarely gets worse. In fact, the chances are high that the terms will improve on the buyer's return.

Adjusting the pace of a negotiation may also depend on the strengths or weaknesses of your position. If you feel that some vulnerability in your position might be exposed, speed up the pace and move on to other issues. On the other hand, if you are on solid ground and feel you are in a good position to change your opponent's position, slow the negotiation down and spend more time on a particular point.

The momentum of a negotiation is another important element to consider. When a deal is moving toward a favorable agreement, the last thing you want to do is slow the pace. Any research, number crunching, or altering of your position should be delegated to members of your negotiating team or support staff. When things seem to be falling into place, keep the negotiation moving in a positive direction. If you have been waiting several weeks to get a physician group to meet with you on a proposed deal, consider moving the negotiations along in a fast and productive fashion. If you interrupt the process at this point, you might find yourself waiting several more weeks before you can resume negotiations, or at worst, you may have to start again.

Developing patience and a sense of timing is critical to your success as a negotiator. Having the proper instincts of when to say something, offer a concession, or change the pace of a negotiation will be one of the most useful techniques you can use at the bargaining table. One of the best ways you can sharpen your sense of timing is to review your past negotiations. Ask yourself what you said or did that had the maximum effect and desired influence on your opponent. This analysis will help you to improve your sense of timing and encourage you to develop a higher level of patience.

DEADLINES

Closely related to the timing of negotiations will be the presence of deadlines. In many negotiations one or both parties will be facing deadlines that must be met. Deadlines can be useful for motivating movement, bringing closure to the process, or forcing a resolution. By understanding how to use a deadline, or deal with a deadline, you will be able to adjust the timing of the negotiation in your favor.

The purpose of using deadlines in a negotiation is to force your opponent to move through his or her range of settlement to consummate an agreement before the deadline expires. A deadline will not cause an opponent to move beyond a settlement range but will simply force them to move faster. By using deadlines, you can often get multiple concessions out of the opponent without having to make concessions yourself. Deadlines can also be used to reduce the opponent's options. Without a deadline, your opponent has an opportunity to shop around for a better deal. You may find yourself in a defensive bargaining position.

When setting a deadline, try to set the shortest deadline you can reasonably justify. While too short a deadline may make your opponent angry, a deadline that is too remote will not provide motivation to act quickly. Adjusting the length of the deadline may be required based on particular circumstances or the experience and confidence of the opponent. Typically, more experienced and competent negotiators will be willing to work with shorter deadlines.

Be prepared to offer a legitimate reason for the deadline. Explain that you need time to deal with other interested parties (you are generating competition for your business and creating a fear of loss in the opponent), or you have other business to handle and want to settle this issue as soon as possible. The stronger your arguments for setting the deadline, the more likely the opponent will respond to it and at the same time not be angered.

Effective deadlines need to involve negative consequences if the deadline is not met. Advise the opponent on the consequences and explain that if a deal cannot be reached by the deadline, you will seek another supplier or alternative proposal. In the case of labor negotiations, the strike deadline includes the threat to the employer of disrupting his business if the agreement is not made in time. When imposing deadlines be prepared to live with the consequences if the opponent does not respond to your deadline. In some cases, failure to meet the deadline may result in no agreement. Do not use deadlines unless you are willing to accept this result. Also, granting your opponent an extension on a deadline must be based on a reasonable explanation. If you grant extensions for little or no reason, your deadlines will not be effective.

On the other hand, it is quite common to find yourself facing a deadline. Sometimes the opponent places a deadline on you, and sometimes deadlines are self-imposed. When an opponent places a deadline, the first question to ask is whether the deadline is real or not. Many deadlines are imposed to force a move or a decision. Everyone has heard from a salesperson that, "the deal is only good for today," or "we have a price increase that will take effect at the beginning of next month." Be skeptical about such deadlines as many of these deals will still be available after the deadline expires. Consider the effect of the threat of backing up the deadline on your organization.

In dealing with an opponent's deadline, ask for more time than you need. Even if you concede this extended deadline, you may still get enough time to negotiate a more favorable agreement. Attempt to get the opponent to agree to a negotiating schedule with identified milestone events or decision points. This can serve to put deadlines on both parties and not just on your side. If possible, place a deadline on the opponent that is prior to his or her deadline. For instance, a common technique used by health plans is to advise providers that they must have a negotiated agreement before they can be advertised in the provider booklet supplied to members. The "provider booklet publishing deadline" has been effective in getting providers to quickly negotiate agreements that may not be in their best interests. If you are a valued member of the provider network, however, consider that they will need your agreement prior to "open enrollment" periods when they are marketing their product. By re-adjusting your negotiating schedule closer to these marketing deadlines, you might find that your opponent will feel pressured to reach an agreement with you.

Another example involves hospital-based physician contracts. In many cases, physicians are hesitant to renegotiate or renew their agreements in advance of the expiration date. While the hospital executive looks at a possible disruption of services, the physicians have the option of either taking a short vacation or simply working under a temporary arrangement. Physicians may delay their negotiations until the eleventh hour and the hospital negotiators may make significant concessions under the pressure of the deadline. One hospital CEO suggested that he now inserts a new clause in all of his annual contracts for physician services. This new clause says, "All renewals of annual contracts for services must be consummated 60 days prior to their effective date in order to allow the hospital to seek an alternate supplier if the original supplier is unable or unwilling to perform." With this clause, he has placed a deadline on the physicians 60 days prior to his own deadline, so he will have ample time to find another physician if the negotiations do not progress to an agreement. He reported that physicians now attempt to renegotiate their contracts well in advance of both deadlines so the hospital will not be forced to look at their "competitors."

Self-imposed deadlines will decrease your bargaining power. Sometimes, even a casual remark about your future plans may force you into a deadline. For instance, if you let your opponent know the board wants an agreement by a certain date or will be approving the deal at their next meeting, you have just presented yourself with a deadline. Having to spend dollars budgeted for capital equipment by the end of the fiscal year is another example of a self-imposed deadline. Sometimes, by asking questions such as, "How is business this quarter?" or "When do you plan to introduce this product?," you might get your opponent to impose deadlines on themselves.

SILENCE

During a negotiating session, being silent can be an effective technique. Many people are uncomfortable with silence. It may make them nervous or they may *imagine* their opponent feels nervous, and so they try to fill the void by talking. By staying silent, you can often get the opponent, especially one who is an inexperienced negotiator, to fill in these awkward times by talking. He may reveal additional information about his position or propose new alternatives to keep the discussions moving or simply to alleviate his anxiety.

Staying silent can be very effective when making arguments. After making a strong point, do not dilute it with more words. Similarly, do not attempt to modify or amplify the argument. Work with your team members to stay silent. A common mistake made by negotiating teams is when each team member tries to reinforce or amplify their teammates' statements. This "machine gunning" behavior actually weakens the original argument and seldom force's concession on the side of the opponent. By continuing to talk, your arguments may not sink in.

Similarly, remain silent after the other party has made a point. Do not be impatient and feel a need to respond right away or reveal your position. In many cases, if the opponent is not sure about the argument, the opponent will shift in the face of silence and amend or adjust what he has just proposed. The opponent may also sense disapproval or disappointment in your silence and immediately offer additional concessions in your favor.

ALTERNATIVE POSITIONS

Offering alternative positions during a negotiation has three purposes: to obtain information, to solve a problem, or to break an impasse. In obtaining information, using an alternative is like sending up a "trial balloon." In response to the alternatives you suggest, your opponent could reveal information significant to your position. For example, you might ask a supplier about the price for a less costly alternative product. The price quoted for the alternative could then become your objective in obtaining the original product desired. In another example, by proposing some "what-if" scenarios to a state regulatory agency, you might obtain important information pertinent to both your current application as well as your long-range plans.

Alternatives may also be used in solving problems at the negotiating table. If a suggested alternative is acceptable as a solution to the problem, it eliminates the need for further negotiations. In one instance, a medical center was concerned about the contractor's ability to complete an expansion project on schedule. The hospital wanted to insert a clause in the contract that contained significant liquidated damages for the contractor if the deadline was not met. As an alternative, the contractor proposed hiring an outside project management company that would develop and monitor a detailed project schedule. This alternative alleviated the concerns of the medical center and removed the problem of the burdensome liquidated damages risk to the contractor.

Sometimes, the use of alternative positions can be helpful in breaking a negotiation impasse or deadlock. If your position is not acceptable to the opponent, a negotiator might propose alternative positions on other issues as a way to break the impasse. In union negotiations, the union's basic wage demands are often offset by alternative positions on other economic issues such as cost of living allowances, paid holidays or vacations, or health benefits.

Only offer only those alternatives that you are willing to have accepted. Recognize that you may be exposing your ranges of settlement on certain issues when you propose alternatives. If the opponent does not accept your "horse trading," the opponent may still seek to obtain concessions on the alternative positions.

CONCESSIONS AND TIMING

Concessions are typically used to break an impasse, to win a corresponding concession, or to conclude an agreement. Concessions indicate the negotiator's involvement and desire to reach an agreement. Concessions can also motivate the opponent to change a position. Each time a concession is made, both parties' realities begin to shift in response to the evolving agreement.

Concessions should be used sparingly. Only make a concession after careful consideration, never impulsively. Try to use concessions in a way that maximizes their effectiveness and improves your position in the overall negotiation. Several key points should be remembered concerning when, and how, to use concessions:

1. Get your opponent to make the first concession. (An exception may be in situations where you want to demonstrate your willingness to be conciliatory at the outset and thus motivate the opponent to make concessions as well.)
2. Attempt to get the opponent to concede on issues of major importance to you.
3. When you concede, make your concessions on issues of minor importance to you.
4. For each concession made, try to get one or more concessions from the opponent.
5. Make a large number of small concessions rather than a few large ones.
6. Take your time between concessions. Do not concede easily and make each concession a meaningful event in the mind of your opponent.
7. Keep track of the number, nature, and extent of each sides' concessions. By summarizing these concessions, you may be able to win concessions later in the negotiation.

The best concessions are ones that have little impact on your organization but have great value to your opponent. For example, an information systems supplier was negotiating an agreement with a large medical center. When discussing the payment terms, the vendor expressed a desire for an accelerated payment for the software portion of the purchase because of certain revenue recognition accounting rules that applied to the company's income statement. On the other hand, the vendor was willing to delay payment for the implementation expenses involved in the project. The medical center took advantage of this fact and made a concession to accommodate the vendor's requests. In doing so, the concession cost the medical center very little as the overall dollar flow in the modified payment schedule was not significantly changed. To the vendor, however, this was a significant concession that would later need to be matched by a concession to the medical center.

Consider concessions and their timing in terms of their effects on the expectation levels of the opponent. If you make a large concession quickly, you may be signaling that you are very flexible and will tend to increase your opponent's expectations. On the other hand, if you delay your large concessions and make only small ones initially, the opponent will begin to believe his or her position or vision of reality will most likely have to change. Studies have also shown that concession patterns are very predictable in negotiations. In situations where deadlines do not exist, a party who starts by making a large concession will usually continue making large concessions until agreement is reached. Conversely, the negotiator who makes smaller concessions and draws them out will typically maintain this pattern throughout the negotiation. Understanding this, you can send a significant message to your opponent based on your concessions and their timing.

MAKING YOUR OPPONENT SEEM UNREASONABLE

Occasionally, a negotiator can obtain an advantage by making the opponent appear unreasonable. After granting several small and insignificant concessions, you might claim, "We want to be cooperative and we've made a number of substantial concessions; now, isn't it your turn?" A contractor who wants relief on a project schedule might use this technique. The contractor might agree to absorb a number of small work items, such as change orders, which could require a legitimate increase in project price. The purpose would be to create a situation where you might then appear unreasonable if you did not agree to the contractor's main objective of obtaining schedule relief. A negotiator can use the same technique to obtain information from an opponent who may be withholding information by using a statement like, "All I am trying to do is understand

and substantiate your position. Will you give me the information to do so?" If the opponent refuses, you could argue that the opponent is being unreasonable.

Another variation of this technique is to take the opponent's position and make it appear unreasonable. For instance, you might argue that the proposed rate being offered by a health plan is not only below your costs, but it is less than the plan is paying to other providers. First, suggest the general unfairness of paying providers different rates for the same services. Point out that by not recovering your costs, your future existence as a provider in their network would be doubtful. This reduction in competition among providers would ultimately result in higher rates being paid to the remaining providers in the network.

STRAW ISSUES

Straw issues involves fabricating an issue or taking a minor issue, blowing it out of proportion, and then conceding after a lengthy discussion. By creating a large number of issues, some of which are real and some of which are made of "straw," you can reduce the opponent's expectation level, provide yourself with trading room, and make it easier for the opponent to take a lesser agreement. When the opponent tells the organization that you have agreed to make numerous concessions, the organization will be more likely to approve the overall agreement.

Labor unions commonly use this technique in their negotiations. They often come to the negotiating table with a hundred or more demands. This large number of demands creates an appearance of wide disagreement with management's representatives. The majority of these demands, however, are "straw issues" which will be conceded eventually after much anguish by the union representatives. Accompanying these concessions, however, will be demands for offsetting concessions on the union's real issues.

An opponent may use straw issues by deliberately inflating a position through detectable errors or overstatements that he expects you to find and question. After finding these errors or overstatements, the opponent will make what appear to be concessions, when in fact no concessions have truly been made. The other party, however, will feel satisfied and be less disposed to demand further concessions from the opponent. In yet another variation, negotiators will often create "funny money." A salesperson might claim that she has already invested significant time and resources in demonstrating the product or allowing you to use a demonstration unit. She will then concede this amount as a "significant" concession when, in fact, these costs have already been absorbed by her organization as a normal sales expense.

In using straw issues, some negotiators will bring in experts to support their point, argue about it at length, and finally concede as was intended all along. By role-playing the straw issues, the concessions that are made often appear to be real and will prevent further requests for additional concessions. Healthcare providers will often use this technique by hiring consulting firms to assist in their negotiations with information systems suppliers. The consulting firm will arrive at the negotiating table with hundreds of issues they claim need to be addressed between their client and the vendor. Interestingly, the consulting firms typically have the same "issues list" in almost every buying situation. The information systems suppliers, who have encountered these firms before, know of these issues, (which are mostly minor or irrelevant), and the manner in which they were resolved in past negotiations. (It is necessary however, to allow the consulting firm to raise all the issues to prove their value to their client.) During the negotiation, the suppliers will offset the "straw issue" technique by following an agenda that focuses on the major issues early in the negotiation and prevent the consultant from using the minor issues. Later, the supplier will "allow" the consultant to achieve concessions on the lesser issues in order to look good in front of the client.

When dealing with opponents who are attempting to use straw issues, you might try the following:

1. Identify the opponent's real objectives during the prenegotiation preparation phase.
2. Add your own straw issues to counter those you suspect your opponent has proposed.
3. Adhere to a prearranged agenda and refuse to allow the opponent to add new "straw" issues during the negotiation.

ROLE-PLAYING

Role-playing can be an effective technique during negotiations. Some role-playing has a legitimate purpose and should be planned out prior to the negotiation. Other role-playing techniques, such as the use of a "good guy–bad guy" approach, are merely efforts to use intimidation as a way to modify the opponent's position.

Significant advantages to role-playing exist among a negotiation team's members. When dealing with an equipment supplier, some members of the team take a hard stance on issues such as price, financing, and guarantees. Other members of the team, typically those who will be involved in the post-sale implementation and use of the product, will take a more moderate position to preserve a relationship with the supplier. Attorneys can also be used in specific roles that involve questioning an opponent's arguments, providing legal counsel, or conducting "what if" analyses. Attorneys are also often used as "sacrificial lambs." In this situation, if a negotiator is preparing for an opponent's team who may be bringing a particularly difficult member, possibly an attorney, the negotiator might also choose to bring an attorney to the meeting. During the negotiation, the negotiator's attorney can then "pick a fight" with the opponent's attorney and both can be dismissed from the negotiation room.

Role-playing combined with "scripting" negotiation team members can be effective in achieving a difficult objective. By delivering the same firmly stated message from several members, a team can convince the opponent of the need to agree to that position. For example, one software vendor was adamant about having all licensing agreements drafted by its legal counsel. The position was non-negotiable and often led to deadlocks with potential clients. To avoid this situation, the company developed a script for the various levels in their sales organization. The message set forth the company's position repeatedly in a firm and consistent manner regardless of whether clients were speaking to front-line salespeople, regional managers, group vice presidents, or even the CEO of the company. Everyone heard the same position and arguments about why the company insisted on its position. After hearing this message many times, clients simply "got it in their heads" that this issue was not up for discussion and agreed to the company's stance.

The good guy–bad guy approach takes role-playing to another, more intimidating, level. While one member of the team takes the good guy role, another takes the bad guy role. Typically, the bad guy takes an extreme position and the good guy takes a more moderate and reasonable position—a position toward which the team is actually striving. By disagreeing with his own bad guy and suggesting a more moderate position, the good guy attempts to win the confidence of the opponent and increase the chance of securing an agreement. However, sometimes the bad guy will cause a walkout or deadlock or, ultimately, prevent an agreement from being reached. Also, the individual playing a bad guy role is often cited by the opponent as a problem in reaching an agreement and ejected from the negotiation. (For this reason, your team leader or spokesperson should not take a bad guy role.)

When a negotiator is faced with an opponent using the good guy–bad guy technique, the best response is to ignore it. Another effective response is to identify the technique and let the opponent know you recognize what they are trying to accomplish. After exposure of their role-playing attempt, they will often cease to use it further. Finally, if the bad guy is either too disruptive or insulting, ask that the person be removed or you will be forced to temporarily break off the negotiations.

DIVERSIONS

Diversions can be used in a negotiation to relax tensions, avoid confrontations on a personal basis, or to divert the opponent who may be "boring in" with very searching questions or with arguments on issues that make you feel vulnerable. By moving the discussion in a different direction, you may avoid a confrontation or a concession. Humor is a valuable and effective diversion at the bargaining table. A story or joke, or even a quick "one-liner," can be very useful in relieving tensions and clearing the air. You must be sure, however, that the humor is well taken and not offensive to the parties on the other side of the table.

A reference to some personal interest of the opponent, or to some common experience unrelated to your workday association can be a diversionary tactic. Remarks or questions might offer a sufficient diversions for you to break the opponent's train of thought or to regain the initiative by switching the area of discussion. However, frequent diversions by the opponent can be disruptive to your plan for the negotiation. If the opponent is constantly introducing tangential or irrelevant items, find a way to move the discussion back in the direction you desire by focusing on the agreed-on agenda.

CAUCUSES

Caucuses are a useful negotiating technique. In a complex negotiation, bargaining *should* be 10-percent conference and 90-percent time out. In most business negotiations, however, this time relationship is reversed. Caucuses give the negotiator an opportunity to evaluate the opponent's position in light of additional information or arguments that have been presented, or that had not been anticipated. By caucusing, the negotiating team has time away from the conference table to reevaluate its own position, strategies, or arguments. Reevaluations should not be attempted at the bargaining table, but rather away from the negotiation conference room. This allows both sides the opportunity to consider all aspects of their relative positions calmly and with sufficient time. Further, the team may need to consult with other representatives from the organization to gather additional information or seek approval for a change in strategies or ranges of settlement.

A caucus can also be called whenever the opponent makes a concession or when preparing to make one of your own. By evaluating the significance of the concession privately, the team can evaluate the direction the opponent seems headed and consider its impact on the overall objectives for the agreement. By caucusing prior to offering a concession, the team also builds up the value of the concession in the opponent's mind. After returning from a time out, you can state, "Well, it's a difficult decision for us to make, but how about if we concede to pay a five-percent increase in your rate?" Restoring control and proper communications with the opponent can be another effective way to use a time out. If one member of your team has spoken out of turn, made an insulting remark, or is becoming intractable, a caucus can help restore a more cordial and unemotional atmosphere. Upon returning from your caucus, you can offer an apology or a clarification of your team member's comments as a way to restart your negotiation along more productive lines.

Calling a caucus can also be effective in avoiding polarized positional situations. If the parties have been discussing a particular issue for a long period of time, going over the same arguments, and neither party has been willing to make a concession, a caucus is generally useful. The longer the discussion goes uninterrupted, the more firmly each party will entrench themselves in their position. After a caucus, parties will generally offer movement once they have been able to examine their opponent's position and are not simply engaged in arguing positions back and forth.

With so many important reasons to use caucuses in negotiations, why is their use in negotiations so infrequent? Two primary reasons explain why many negotiators fail to make use of this effective technique. First, a party may feel that a caucus makes it appear that he or she is not fully prepared. By not calling a caucus, negotiators falsely believe they are "saving face." The fact is, a negotiator is never fully prepared or 100-percent certain of all the facts and information prior to a negotiation. Therefore, at some point in every negotiation, *both* parties will enter areas for which they are unprepared and should call for a time out. Teams that are unwilling to face this fact, and instead try to save face, seldom fool anyone and typically expose vulnerabilities that can be exploited by their opponents.

The other reason that caucuses are not frequently used is simply that it delays the negotiation. Many healthcare executives feel pressured to accomplish 80 hours of work in a 40-hour workweek and are hesitant to slow down discussions by taking a break. While they may accomplish some time savings during the bargaining phase of the agreement, the savings will evaporate very quickly during the implementing of a poorly developed agreement.

WALKOUTS AND DEADLOCKS

On occasion, walkouts or the threat of a walkout can be an advantage, but not without some risk. The old phrase, "Never buy a car without walking off the lot once," contains some wisdom. The risk of a walkout is that it may be very difficult to get the negotiations started again and back on track. When a walkout leads to the opponent making a compromise, it is a successful technique. When the walkout fails, however, reconciliation will be difficult and your position weakened. A walkout should be carefully considered when the opponent has become intransigent or further arguments would be wasteful. If you believe the opponent will see the walkout as a clear indication that he needs to lower his expectations and change positions, then this technique may be appropriate. On the other hand, if the opponent perceives it as a termination of the discussions, or a theatrical ploy, the technique will seldom succeed and should be avoided.

If you reach a point in the negotiation where a walkout by the opponent is imminent, try to forestall it. Suggest a recess or break, maybe even overnight, so both parties have time to think things over and review positions. Other times, it may be best to let the opponent walk, let him know of the losses both parties will suffer if no agreement is reached, and then try to get together later. In either event, remain cordial and friendly and express a willingness to reopen the negotiations after the opponent has had time to reconsider. Do not allow a walkout by the opponent to force you into making unsupported concessions.

Closely related to walkouts are deadlocks. By terminating the negotiations without agreement, a negotiator can often achieve concessions or gain information about the opponent's limits for final settlement. A deadlock can be very effective if the negotiator has the patience to let it work, has the support of the organization, and is in a superior bargaining position. Health plans have used deadlocks effectively when negotiating agreements with providers. If the health plan has delivered significant business to a provider in the past, the potential of lost revenues will often force providers to make significant concessions. As long as the plan has other suitable providers in its network, the loss of any particular provider may only be a minor consequence.

Deadlocks can also indicate poor communications between the two parties. Sometimes neither party considers the fact that its own best interest depends on understanding and accommodating the interests of the opponent. When encountering a deadlock, consider listening more and talking less. Like walkouts, deadlocks can be broken most often by a calm and reasonable attitude. When you are faced with a deadlock, offer an acceptable alternative, make a concession to the opponent's terms, or terminate your negotiation.

Obviously, of the three it would be better to find an acceptable alternative.

Walkouts and deadlocks are high-risk negotiating techniques. If a negotiator is either unprepared to handle the high risks or unwilling to accept the consequence of terminating the negotiation, neither of these techniques is appropriate.

FINAL OFFERS

Another high-risk negotiating technique is the use of a final offer. Final offers are intended to bring closure to a negotiation either with or without an agreement. A final offer may be used when a negotiator has reached the end of the range of settlement and can move no further. A final offer can also be effective when further negotiations do not justify your additional time and effort or when you wish to either conclude the negotiation or move on to an alternative. Final offers are also used effectively in negotiations where a deadline is at issue.

A final offer is essentially a "take it or leave it" position. Consequently, it generally leaves a negative impression on the opponent and can result in hard feelings. When possible, you should consider trying to dress up your final offer by offering concessions on minor terms or straw issues, holding out promises for future business, or emphasizing the reasonableness of your final offer. If you truly need an agreement with this opponent, a final offer should not be used. Your final offer should mean just that—it is final. Expressing any flexibility is a mistake and would cause future final offers to be ignored.

CLOSING

When you are confident that both sides have reached agreement on all points, move to close the agreement. When is the "best" time to close the agreement? Although no specific time will work in every negotiation, the key question is whether you believe the opponent will say "yes." If you are not sure if the time is right, continue bargaining, perhaps by explaining the last counteroffer, or by asking questions of the opponent regarding the offer or counteroffer. If the opponent is wavering, assure him that you believe that the agreement is in both party's mutual interest and are confident both sides are receiving a good deal. If the opponent is still reluctant to say, "it's a deal," begin talking about the wording of the contract. Your intent to enter into an agreement may be clearer and provide the push needed for a final acceptance. Also, a question like, "When would you like to begin work?" might provide the catalyst needed to achieve final agreement.

Do not appear too anxious to close. If you appear too forceful in trying to get the opponent to say "yes," he may get suspicious and ask for more time to reexamine the deal. The art of closing is based on the presumption that you want to get an agreement at this point and your whole attitude projects it. Your negotiating efforts were designed to get to this point. A good negotiator will seize the opportunity and exhibit a conviction that the agreement is in the best interests of both parties and it is fair and reasonable.

CHAPTER 7

Common Negotiating Situations

A NEGOTIATOR WILL face many negotiating situations in a career. In previous chapters, the process, strategies, and techniques for negotiating have been described. Your skill as a negotiator will involve assessing each situation and adapting these concepts in the most effective manner. However, several types of negotiating situations are common, including three-way negotiations, mediation, telephone negotiations, and monopoly situations.

THREE-WAY NEGOTIATIONS

Some negotiating situations have more than two parties at the negotiating table. The presence of additional parties may create increased conflict. Usually, efforts should be directed at reducing the number of parties represented. However, more than two distinct sides to a negotiation may be necessary, for example, a three-party negotiation might involve a health plan, a group of physicians, and a hospital. In other cases, the parties might include a supplier, a department head or end user, and the finance or purchasing department. Or, in other instances, the board, medical staff, and administrative team might be involved. In all of these situations, a good negotiator will develop a strategy for accomplishing his or her objectives as well as those of the other parties.

Three-way negotiations are inherently unstable and will commonly become a two-on-one situation. Generally, two of the parties will see a benefit in aligning their efforts, often at the expense of the third party. In the case of a health plan-physician-hospital situation, health plans have been successful in aligning interests with physicians and using them to play one hospital against another to lower the hospital's reimbursement rates. Suppliers typically try to align themselves with end users with the hope of building enough momentum to overcome any resistance by the financial or purchasing personnel. Healthcare executives will often seek support of their boards "behind the scenes" before engaging in a three-way negotiation that includes members of the medical staff. Aligning with another party is simply an effort to increase bargaining power. When you "partner" with another party, you pick up the bargaining power of the stronger partner. For this reason, you will always want to pick your partner. Seldom will a party benefit from being the odd-man out.

In a three-way negotiation, natural forces may cause two parties to align their interests. When hospitals and physicians have perceived health plans as a "common enemy," efforts at uniting their sides have included the establishment of physician-hospital organizations (PHOs), practice acquisitions, or other integrative models. Although many of these efforts may have failed due in part to unresolved conflicting interests between the hospitals and physicians, the intent in gaining bargaining power was certainly there. Hospital boards and their executive teams have often joined forces when dealing with medical staff members they feel exhibit too much self-interest at the expense of the hospital organization.

In other situations, an active strategy can be pursued to achieve a two-on-one advantage. Sales representatives will frequently ignore hospital visitation policies requiring them to check in with the purchasing department prior to meeting with end users. By avoiding the purchasing personnel, the sales representative seeks to align with the interests of the end user before the purchasing/finance and end-user personnel can get together. At the negotiating table, this situation often results in an unfortunate two-on-one with the hospital's purchasing personnel sitting in an inferior bargaining position. In other situations, a physician will often place a middle of the night call to a board member to solicit her support in advance of upcoming negotiations with the hospital's executive team.

In one case, a three-way negotiation became a two-on-one negotiation when a contractor, an architect, and a hospital were trying to determine the responsibility for payment to repair the leaky roof on a new hospital building. Based on all the information available, it was unclear which of the parties was at fault for the problem. The contractor felt the problem was due to architectural errors, and the architect claimed the problem was due to faulty construction. To further complicate matters, the leaks had occurred during a torrential rainstorm with record amounts of precipitation. The contractor was in a poor bargaining position because it was still owed a substantial sum of money for the job and was responsible for the actions of the roofing subcontractor. The architect, on the other hand, was in a more favorable position as he had already been paid for his work and had an architectural services agreement with the hospital that cleared him of any responsibility for his own errors. Meanwhile, the hospital was in the best bargaining position as it had considerable amounts of future work scheduled and could threaten both the architect and the contractor with eliminating their firms from consideration on any future projects.

The contractor recognized his poor bargaining position and developed a strategy to align with the hospital. During the negotiation, the contractor offered to do the repair work at cost with no profit, and further offered to pay a small percentage of the repair costs. At this point, the hospital representative asked the architect what he was willing to offer. The architect responded that he did not believe the leaky roof was his fault and he was not prepared to offer anything until evidence was presented that proved his culpability. From the hospital's perspective, the contractor suddenly looked like he was trying to be part of a solution while the architect appeared to remain part of the problem. Very quickly, a two-on-one negotiation was created with the hospital and contractor working together against the architect. The architect eventually paid for a large majority of the repair work.

MEDIATION

When two parties are unable to reach agreement, mediation may be required. An informal mediation may take place where a superior seeks to facilitate an agreement between two subordinates, or a more formal mediation may occur with an outside, third-party serving as a mediator. Mediation is a process where the mediator ascertains the overlapping ranges of settlement and proposes a solution within that overlap. A successful mediator needs to have strong questioning and listening skills to discern the interests and ranges of settlement for each party.

Important to note, however, is that a mediator is never totally impartial and every mediator has biases or prejudices and a sense of fairness. Asking a physician to mediate the dispute between a medical staff and a hospital board would probably not offer a completely impartial situation, but neither would use of a nonphysician mediator. A superior might be fair and unbiased in mediating a dispute between two subordinates but would certainly have a personal interest in the solution.

When asked to assume the role of mediator, ask yourself the question, "Do I really need to do this?" In many cases, the dispute may be coming to you simply because one party or the other is unable or unwilling to negotiate. In such cases, the better course of action is to put the problem back on the two parties with instructions to work it out between themselves. However, a dispute between a board and medical staff that could result in a deadlock may require intervention.

A danger of serving as a mediator is the potential for the mediator to become part of the solution. In the case of the leaky roof, some may suggest that the hospital representative should act as a mediator between the architect and contractor. Since the hospital has a vested interest in the solution, the possibility of the hospital putting up part of the costs to repair the roof becomes more likely if the other two parties are not willing to assume the full cost of repairs. As a first step to mediating the dispute, establish that the hospital is not at fault for the leaky roof and should not be responsible for any repair costs. With these facts established, the hospital is in a much safer role to act as a mediator to get the two parties to agree on what portion of the repair costs each is willing to pay.

A successful mediator proposes a solution. While initially the mediator may want to facilitate discussions between the two parties, at some point an agreement must be reached to bring the mediation to a close. After listening to both sides carefully, suggest a solution that is both fair and reasonable. The hospital representative with the leaky roof might suggest, "I do not believe we will ever find out who is at fault for the leaky roof. Therefore, I feel it is fair and reasonable for both of you to contribute equally to the cost of repairs. This is not, for either of you, an admission of guilt, but it will go a long way in making sure both of you are considered for any future work with our hospital." By proposing a solution and applying some additional pressure through the use of a threat, both the architect and contractor would be reluctant to decline the proposed solution. By rejecting your "fair and reasonable" solution, either party would risk identifying you, their customer, as somehow being unfair or unreasonable.

TELEPHONE NEGOTIATIONS

Negotiations that would never be possible face to face because of inconvenience, timing, or geographic distance are made possible by the use of a telephone. The telephone offers convenience, speed, accessibility, and low cost. With the development of cellular phones, negotiations can take place anytime and anywhere.

A telephone negotiation has several advantages:

1. Speed—The telephone is usually the fastest way to get in touch with an opponent if the situation requires quick resolution.
2. Convenience—A telephone negotiation does not requre travel to another office or location, especially when using cellular phones.
3. Privacy—In a telephone netotiation, your opponent is unable to "read" your physical reactions to his arguments, and is also unaware of other members of your negotiating team who may be present on the call.
4. Impersonal—When dealing with an opponent who may use threatening or intimidating techniques, standing firm is easier over a telephone then in person. It is easier to say "no" over the phone.

Some disadvantages are:

1. Pace—Because of the speed at which telephone negotiations often take place, the pace of the negotiations is typically very fast and may, in many cases, be rushed.
2. Preparation—Negotiations can be initiated quickly and the process may be started without proper preparation.
3. Privacy—You are unable to read the opponent's physical reactions to your arguments. You are also unaware of other members of your opponent's negotiating team who may be present on the call.
4. Impersonal—Developing strong personal relationships over the telephone is difficult. The opponent may take a tougher stance or find it easier to say "no" over the phone.

The primary danger in telephone negotiations is lack of notice. In a "cold calling" situation, one party is not adequately prepared to begin the negotiation process. Telemarketers use this technique to their advantage. *The vast majority of unprepared negotiations take place on a telephone.*

Telephone negotiations will represent a sizable portion of the situations you encounter, and a skilled negotiator will take advantage of this valuable device. The following suggestions might be helpful in avoiding the disadvantages of telephone negotiations:

1. Be prepared—If someone calls to negotiate and you are not prepared, delay the negotiation if at all possible. Suggest that you are willing to discuss the issue but have a couple of pressing matters to take care of first. Schedule a mutually agreeable time to call back, and spend the interim preparing.

2. Slow the process down—Be aware that telephone negotiations tend to move at a quicker pace than other negotiating situations. Many times, the opponent will be seeking immediate decisions or commitments. Recognize that patience and a slower pace will be to your benefit. Defer certain issues or decisions with statements like, "I can't make a decision until I have had a chance to review the data or documents," or "I will have to check with my colleagues on that issue and get back to you." The use of the "pregnant pause" or silence technique is especially effective on the telephone.

3. Build relationships first—If developing a personal relationship will be a benefit to the negotiation, consider using telephone negotiations only in the later stages of the process. By engaging in some face-to-face discussions first, the two parties can develop the feelings of trust that can later be used on the telephone. In dealing with regulatory agencies, pay them a visit in person before trying to negotiate agreements over the phone.

MONOPOLY SITUATIONS

Negotiating with an opponent who enjoys monopoly (or "quasi-monopoly") status is a very challenging situation. Without the ability to generate competition or alternatives, a negotiator is faced with an opponent with vastly superior bargaining power. The opponent could be a pharmaceutical manufacturer with the only drug of its kind on the market, a hospital-based physician group that has an exclusive contract, an equipment supplier who has maneuvered itself into a sole-source position, or a physician group that may be the only provider of a particular specialty. The negotiator must reach agreement with the other party or suffer severe negative consequences. Meanwhile, the opponent is often in a position to make a take it or leave it offer at any time. Focus your efforts on negotiating a more favorable agreement *before* the take it or leave it offer is put on the table as well as confronting this final demand if, and when, it is made.

Prioritize and Focus Objectives

Before entering into a monopoly negotiation, focus and prioritize your objectives. Identify those issues and concessions that will be the most important and *focus* your limited bargaining power in achieving those goals while leaving the remaining issues to be resolved in the opponent's favor. This "lowering of expectations" should not be construed as exhibiting a defeatist attitude but rather a realistic setting of achievable goals that will be valuable to your organization. By entering the negotiation demanding significant concessions on *all* issues, your "unrealistic" expectations may cause the opponent to take an equal and opposite position. Unfortunately, the opponent's demands for major concessions on all issues can often be backed up with superior bargaining power.

Also, consider the opponent's objectives and priorities. What are the main issues and positions the opponent wants to resolve? Are you able to accept the opponent's positions on those issues? If the positions are not acceptable, a deadlock or no agreement is likely. On the other hand, if you can live with those positions, you may want to consider accepting them and looking for concessions on other issues of lesser importance to the opponent. For example, a health plan that has 50 percent of the market share will probably not be negotiating its position on reimbursement rates. If you are willing to accept their rate after some argument, the plan's representatives may be willing to make concessions in the areas of medical management, claims submission, or benefit eligibility. Therefore, consider where you want to fight your battles and understand that your agreement to their major issues and positions is probably inevitable.

Build Bargaining Power

Do not enter a monopoly situation feeling that you have no bargaining power. You always have some. The primary ways of building bargaining power in a monopoly negotiation are to gather information, appeal to reasonableness, tie the agreement to other business, or use third parties.

Gather Information

The best way to build bargaining power in a monopoly negotiation is to gather as much information as possible prior to the negotiation. Possessing sound logical arguments backed up with facts, figures, or other information makes it difficult for the opponent to issue non-negotiable demands without appearing unreasonable. Comparing the opponent's position with established industry standards may point out inadequacies in the offer. Competitive offers, even if they are not an option, are valuable insight into what a reasonable agreement might be. Talking to others who have negotiated with the opponent may reveal important information regarding strategies, techniques, and issues. Some questions to ask colleagues are, "If you were to renegotiate your agreement with Company X, what would you want to change in terms of your strategies, issues, or timing? What are its strengths or weaknesses? What are the biggest problems you had with your agreement with Company X?"

The other information you want to calculate is the best alternative to a negotiated agreement (BATNA). The BATNA allows you to establish a lower end on your range of settlement as well as give you an estimate of the negative consequences if no agreement is reached. Also, calculate the negative consequences for the opponent if an agreement is not reached. A loss in revenues, loss in market share, elimination of future business opportunities, or forcing you to look at other competing products are arguments that can be used to convince the opponent to be more flexible. Think about resources you have that your opponent desires. If your opponent is a physician, you might possess equipment or services required for his practice, or affiliation with your organization may be desirable to increase his patient base.

Appeal to Reasonableness

Presented with factual evidence and strong logical arguments, most opponents are reasonable people. Justify your vision of reality with the information gathered during the prenegotiation preparation.

Tie the Current Negotiation to Other Business Opportunities

It may be useful to let the opponent know that an intractable stance may affect other business opportunities between both parties. Suggest that while you recognize that you are over the barrel in this particular situation, you might choose to look elsewhere for other products that you are currently buying from his company. However, this threat is a high-risk, conflict-escalating technique and is better used later in the negotiation process. Alternatively, attempt to tie the opponent's concessions in the current negotiation with the potential for future business.

Use Third Parties

Taking advantage of the greater bargaining power of a third party may assist you in achieving concessions you might not otherwise attain. In one example, a hospital was having difficulty getting its anesthesiologist group to negotiate reasonable rates for their services. Because of the monopoly they had on the market, the anesthesiologists had taken a hard-line stance in dealing with the hospital. The hospital CEO looked to his medical staff as a valuable third party to help break the impasse. He was able to convince several physicians who used the anesthesiologists' services that their interests were at risk if a reasonable agreement could not be reached with the hospital-based physicians. These physicians then approached the anesthesiologists and urged them to reconsider their positions. The physicians also let the anesthesiologists know that while they would prefer to keep the current group at the hospital, seeking an alternate anesthesiology group was an option they were willing to consider. Faced with this prospect of potential competition, the anesthesiology group became willing to compromise on several of their demands.

One other strategy that is helpful in these situations is to remember that there is always another negotiation. While you may be forced into accepting positions that are not to your liking in the current agreement, you can lay the groundwork for achieving further concessions at the negotiating table next time. You might suggest that while you will be willing to accept a rate lower than you need in the current agreement, you would also like to tie future reimbursement rates to your performance. You might propose increased reimbursement tied to lowered utilization rates, increased patient satisfaction scores, or improved quality outcomes. Often, your opponent will concede to these requests as they cost him little or nothing to give away in the current negotiation. For you, however, it will substantially increase your bargaining power for the next round of negotiations with that opponent.

One unique situation in some healthcare negotiations is a request by suppliers for a "preferred vendor" or "vendor select" designation prior to negotiations. In essence, the supplier is asking for the exclusive right to negotiate with the client *for a limited period of time.* After giving the supplier this status, the client agrees not to discuss a deal with any other competing firms during this period. The suppliers contend that they are able to offer a better deal quickly without fear of the client shopping the offer to other competing entities. If competitors are present, suppliers suggest that they must hold something back to make further concessions when they get a last look at the deal.

As a customer, would you ever designate a supplier as "vendor select" and thus create a monopoly negotiation? Quite possibly. First, the negotiator may be in a situation where the relationship with the supplier is more important than any particular outcome. In the case of an information systems supplier, the hard dollar costs of purchasing a system are often minor compared to the value of a strong working relationship between the two organizations. While the loss of competitive pressure may result in a higher initial price, the good relationship gained might provide a very good return for this additional expense. Generating true competition is another element to consider. In many cases, the supplier already enjoys a quasi-monopoly status with your organization based on compatibility issues, standardization, end-user preference, and other factors. While you might attempt to generate competition, the bargaining power associated with your efforts would be minor. Finally, in situations where you are trying to develop a long-term, mutually beneficial "partnership," giving a supplier "preferred vendor" status may send an important message. While it goes against the grain for most negotiators to ever sacrifice bargaining power by not generating competition, there are certainly times when this strategy may be considered.

CHAPTER 8

Challenging
Negotiating Situations

WHILE EVERY NEGOTIATION you have engaged in has probably been unique, several situations present challenges to successfully
achieving good agreements. The purpose of this chapter is to examine a few of these challenging situations and discuss ways in which
you can deal with them effectively. Some situations that may be encountered are dealing with conflict, handling non-negotiators or opponents who are unwilling to concede, and managing the "hardball"
negotiator.

CONFLICT IN NEGOTIATIONS

Conflict is often characterized as a struggle over values or claims to
scarce status, power, or resources. Negotiation is therefore a natural breeding ground for conflict. During conflict, the aims of the opponents are to neutralize, dominate, or eliminate their rivals. Many
healthcare negotiations will necessarily involve conflict as discussions entail agreement over budgets, payment for services, or job positions. Skillful negotiators view conflict as a natural occurrence in
any organization. They seek to understand the sources of conflict,

Figure 8.1: The Sicilian Stalemate

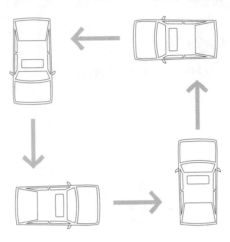

conflict escalators that can occur during the negotiation process, and conflict de-escalators that can be used to resolve conflicts. Further, they understand their own tendencies in dealing with conflict.

One danger of conflicts is that the parties get locked into a position where they surrender everything or surrender more than they should because they have not learned how to deal with conflict productively. An inability to resolve conflict is illustrated by a drawing referred to as "the Sicilian stalemate." Figure 8.1 depicts four automobiles that have arrived at an intersection at the same time with a malfunctioning traffic light. Each car's progress is blocked by another car. It would, of course, be a relatively simple matter for one of the cars to back up and let another car pass and allow the remaining motorists to have free passage. The point of the drawing is that negotiators sometimes sacrifice the major interest, that is, getting through the intersection, because they are unwilling to yield on a minor issue such as backing up first. As unreasonable as this approach appears in the context of this illustration, many negotiators behave exactly the same way during conflicts at the bargaining table.

Conflict Is Not Intrinsically Bad

Some negotiators are of the view that conflict is intrinsically bad and is evidence that something is wrong. Many conclude that conflict must be eliminated for the good of the organization. To the successful negotiator, the modern view of conflict is that it is inevitable and not necessarily harmful. In many instances conflict can be used as a catalyst for change and can help in reaching a better agreement. Threatening competition to an existing supplier, for example, may lead to conflict but can also result in the supplier providing increased value by lowering costs or increasing the quality of the product. Conflict can be managed in such a way that losses are minimized and gains maximized. The use of capitation as a reimbursement methodology in the 1990s, for example, created considerable conflict among provider groups. When a multispecialty group of physicians attempted to arrive at the appropriate sub-capitated amounts, each subspecialty tried to claim as large a portion as possible. Once the parties discovered that the overall capitated amount was insufficient to cover all of their respective portions, discussions moved forward in a more productive direction. Physicians have subsequently developed referral guidelines and mechanisms, risk-sharing arrangements, and other means to fairly distribute the available money. The benefit of these creative solutions was an emergence of "true" managed care as providers began working with each other to maximize efficiencies and utilization of resources.

Negotiating parties are competing, and the competition may decide whose values will prevail, such as in the classic mission versus margin discussions in not-for-profit healthcare organizations. In other situations, parties may be competing to gain control over administrative functions, additional funding for programs or equipment, or be vying for the vice presidency of an organization.

When competing at the negotiating table, parties can be in conflict with each other and yet still like each other. In healthcare organizations, departments may be in conflict over resource allocation yet still work together in a congenial manner. Conflict need not be detrimental to the parties involved. When viewed in this light, conflict is not an impediment to developing successful agreements; it is, or can be, a catalyst toward a more aligned and efficient agreement. No matter what type of agreement is being negotiated, conflict should be considered valuable and an opportunity to achieve an overall gain for the parties involved. Suppressing conflict can be costly as the unresolved issues will usually surface later in implementing the negotiated agreement.

Sources of Conflict

During the prenegotiation preparation process, conflict should be anticipated and a strategy developed to leverage it in a constructive fashion. The first step in dealing with conflict is to understand its source. Numerous potential sources of conflict in any negotiation include competition for limited resources, value clashes, issue ambiguity, change, complexity of multiparty negotiations, and stress and pressure.

Competition for Limited Resources

A common source of conflict in any negotiation is when parties compete for limited resources. A physician carving out a larger share of a capitation payment for his own subspecialty is a competition for limited resources. A department head attempting to increase staffing may also create conflict by gaining a larger percentage of the total organization's labor pool. When competing for limited resources, the parties are playing a zero sum game; neither party can increase its position without diminishing that of the other party.

The world we live in offers virtually limitless examples of personal or political conflicts that grow out of clashes of values. Parents think their teenagers should be home at a certain hour, while the adolescent children feel they should be independent and have the freedom to set their own hours.

In a hospital setting, the executive staff thinks of the organization as a "service industry," and efficiency, return on investment, and other performance measures are usually paramount. Other employees of the hospital, such as the clinical staff, view their work as a calling to help the sick and injured, no matter what the cost. Some physicians will subordinate economic considerations to do good, while others are more interested in "doing well." Some hospital employees, such as support personnel, may look on their work as just another job and their focus may be entirely unrelated to medical care.

Consider an example in which a patient complains to a nurse about maintenance employees performing noisy chores late at night. The nurse may feel that it is wrong for the maintenance people to disturb the patient. The maintenance people, however, would argue that they should not have to alter work schedules simply because one patient was bothered. Some physicians might side with the nurse and argue that the patient's comfort is paramount, while other doctors might feel that the patient is a charity case and should not complain. To resolve the issue, hospital administration could solve the problem by moving the patient to another room or rearranging the maintenance employees' chores.

A negotiated agreement must take into account the values of all parties to the conflict or run the risk of inferring that all but one of the parties is "wrong." In conflict caused by value differences, none of the parties should be regarded as wrong. Managing conflict does not involve judging what is right, but rather resolving conflict in such a way that the best interests of the organization— in the last example, the hospital—are served. Accepting this point of view is important for negotiators. In a negotiation involving conflict over values, the concept of right and wrong is irrelevant. Typically, each party regards his own values as right and the other party's as wrong. Values always make perfect sense to the people who profess them. Conflict will arise when we project our values onto the other party.

Ambiguity

Lack of detail surrounding issues or high levels of ambiguity are another important source of conflict. Negotiating a joint venture agreement without a clear identification of the venture's objectives or the resources that will be available is difficult. Trying to agree on a reimbursement rate for a provider without some projections regarding patient volumes, or approaching a physician concerning her practice patterns without strong supporting data and possible practice guidelines will seldom yield the desired results.

Failure to define the rules and the responsibilities of each party in an agreement will lead to further conflict downstream. A capital equipment supplier may view its role in the organization primarily as "selling" customers. The production staff may view its scope of services as manufacturing the product. What happens when a customer wants a clinical demonstration and a tour of the manufacturing plant? Without clearly defined roles that anticipate such scenarios, conflict will arise as neither party would view such an activity to be within their respective responsibility.

In healthcare negotiations, a fair number of assumptions are made about what will happen in the future regarding the marketplace, competition, evolving technologies, and disease patterns. These assumptions introduce an element of ambiguity at the negotiating table, for one party's estimates may vary considerably from those of the opponent's. The parties should stay away from negotiating what the right assumptions might be and, alternatively, focus on negotiating an agreement flexible enough to anticipate future change. The use of formulas as a basis for modifying the agreement is a good solution. For example, a new HMO entering a hospital's marketplace may ask for pricing of services to accommodate the needs of its future members which it projects to be 20,000 enrollees in 12 months. The hospital may be skeptical of this market penetration figure since there are already several well-established managed care plans in the market area. Rather than trying to negotiate what the HMO's likely enrollment numbers will be, the hospital might negotiate an agreement where the pricing would change based on the actual number of members that are enrolled.

Reaction to Change

The prospect of change is present in every negotiating situation, indeed, the very purpose of a negotiation is to implement change within the organization or industry. Most individuals, even those who consider themselves flexible, have difficulty dealing with change. Change is difficult for people because they have invested considerable efforts in arranging circumstances as they currently exist. A physician may have spent a considerable portion of his life attaining his current position of prestige, recognition, and economic status. Significant resistance or conflict will arise when proposing any change in the status quo. When the Clinton administration proposed massive healthcare reform during its first term, the conflict that arose was enormous. Although almost all sectors of the healthcare industry agreed that some change was necessary, they opposed the massive reforms proposed by the administration.

Not all individuals react to change in a similar way. Some believe that the adaptable will ultimately prosper in healthcare. These "change promoters" are often recognized for their entrepreneurial ideas and bring imagination and creativity to the negotiating table. Other people are "change resisters" who believe that maintaining the present situation is the preferred alternative. Others fear change simply because of a fear of the unknown. This was the case for many physicians when the idea of capitated reimbursement was first introduced. When both a "change promoter" and a "change resister" are present at the negotiating tale, conflict will arise.

Complexity in Multiparty Negotiations

Opportunities for conflict also arise due to the complexity of multiple-party negotiations. It is considerably easier to address needs and interests when only two parties are at the bargaining table. Opportunities for conflict increase substantially when introducing multiple parties to the negotiation who will all be affected in some manner by the eventual agreement, as in the example of the Clinton administration's health reform efforts.

Multiple parties as a force for escalating conflict in negotiations is easily seen during planning and budgeting efforts. While a department head will be easily able to decide and rationalize the allocation of human and financial resources in his or her own department, the same decisions become more difficult and conflict will escalate as numerous managers and executives get involved at the organizational level. At the system level, conflict can further escalate with multiple organizations trying to agree on issues of strategic direction or capital planning.

The Stress and Pressure Involved in Negotiations

The stress and pressure that participants may feel during a negotiation is another source of conflict. The need for economic security and prosperity are a major source of stress to many in healthcare today. Many physicians who once enjoyed significant income levels have experienced a constant erosion of revenues over the last decade. To augment their current incomes, physicians feel pressure to enter into contracts they previously avoided, to initiate new ventures involving greater risks, and to compromise much of the lifestyle they have come to enjoy. Additionally, to contract successfully with health plans, physicians are finding it necessary to affiliate with their colleagues by joining IPAs, medical groups, or health systems rather than continue the independent practice of medicine they anticipated when entering the profession. With an uncertain future, these individuals feel considerable stress and pressure to make the right choices without having adequate information. As one physician pointed out, "I am being forced to play a game where the rules have yet to be established."

Much has been written on the stressful environment of today's healthcare marketplace. For many, a 40-hour workweek has been long forgotten. Coupled with the demands of the profession are increased responsibilities to families and other nonwork related activities. In this environment, most individuals experience some level of stress. During a negotiation, proposing to increase the job responsibilities for a department head will enhance the level of stress and will often result in a conflict.

Conflict Escalators

While conflict during negotiations is inevitable, a skillful negotiator will carefully monitor the situation for conflict escalators. Virtually all major conflicts start as minor ones. The escalation of a minor conflict to a major one is usually the result of the actions of the parties, often unknowingly or unintentionally, while attempting to deal with the conflict. Conflict escalators tend to be emotional reactions to conflict and can possibly destroy any opportunity for agreement. By looking for conflict escalators during the negotiation process, a negotiator may be able to intervene before the conflict becomes unmanageable or destructive. Some examples of the most common conflict escalators are mirror images, differing interpretations of the same facts or behavior, double standards, polarized positions, enemy images, or over simplification.

Mirror Images

When each party regards the other's position as essentially opposite to his own position, a mirror image situation occurs. For example, a health plan might present its medical management program as a process to provide appropriate services to members. On the other hand, providers would view the medical management program as the health plan's attempt to deny necessary care. As a result, both parties are blind to opportunities for accommodation or compromise and will try to reinforce their own perceptions.

Different Interpretations of the Same Facts or Behavior

In a situation of differing interpretations, each party sees only what they wish to see. In one instance, a health plan had proposed a five-cent per month increase on a per member per month (PMPM) basis to a mental health provider. This amount would have raised their monthly PMPM payment to $1.25 from $1.20. The provider, on the other hand, felt that an increase of 10 cents per member per month was a more appropriate amount. The provider stated, "It is only one nickel per member per month. What's the big deal?" The health plan negotiator responded, "It may only be one nickel per member per month, but if you apply that increase to all of our members, it is a $2.6 million increase in our medical costs." This difference in perspective was over a five-cent issue. Some nursing personnel believe that some physicians' behavior toward the nursing staff is both unprofessional and demeaning. When asked about this, physicians often reply that they are merely providing instructions to the nurse to ensure proper patient care. What seemed to be simple instructions given by the physician came across to the nurse as an insult.

Double Standards

Conflict can also escalate when one party judges his own acts or positions by different standards than he uses to judge his opponent's acts or positions. The opponent may believe that this incongruity is evidence that the other party is unilaterally changing the rules in his own favor. For example, hospital executives and hospital personnel may differ about the appropriate "gifts and gratuities" policies for dealing with salespeople. The executives may believe that the gifts and gratuities are intended to "buy" the hospital's business and should be declined. Hospital employees, on the other hand, may believe that gift and gratuities are essentially the same as the hospital providing its medical staff with free meals, preferential parking, continuing medical education, support services, and so forth. To continue to argue a position after the double standard has been identified can be a significant conflict escalator.

Polarized Single-Issue Positions

During some conflicts, parties tend to focus on a single issue and adopt positions that they are unwilling to concede. By digging into their positions and refusing to compromise, agreement is difficult, if not impossible, to achieve. With both parties taking an "It's my way or the highway" attitude, their efforts tend to focus on trying to force the opponent into surrendering. One instance where this occurred was in a union negotiation between a hospital and its registered nurses, who were represented by a state nursing association. On the issue of union representation, the hospital repeatedly proclaimed that it would maintain its current "open shop" status. Meanwhile, the negotiating team leader for the nurses had made a commitment to the members that he would achieve a "union shop" concession at the bargaining table. While the hospital made significant concessions in terms of wages, benefits, and work rules, it was unwilling to make any concession on its "open shop" requirement.

Unfortunately, many of the rank-and-file members' expectations were focused on getting just such a concession. The nurses failed to recognize what was otherwise a very good agreement, and they eventually went on strike for almost three months. During the strike, the hospital was able to continue operating with its nonunion nurses and suffered only a minor loss in terms of profitability. In fact, after realizing it was not being hurt economically, the hospital decided to simply "wait out" the union and withdrew many of the concessions it had offered on other parts of the contract. Eventually, the strike ended with a new contract that was less than what the hospital had originally offered and failed to include the "union shop" provision. By focusing their attention almost solely on the representation issue, the nurses failed to see what could have been a favorable agreement in almost all other areas. Had both sides been willing to look for some middle ground, for example, an "agency shop" provision, a gain-gain opportunity might have been found.

Polarized positions often result when one or both parties fail to develop an appropriate range of settlement. Without a range of settlement, concessions are highly unlikely. If the other party is unwilling to accept such a position, the unyielding party will be left in a polarized situation. A good negotiator will be very cautious in using negotiating phrases such as "this issue is non-negotiable" or "not accepting our position on this issue will be a deal-breaker." Unless you *really* require agreement on an issue, you risk considerable conflict escalation and a possible deadlock.

The Opponent as the Enemy

Viewing the opponent as an enemy is another conflict escalator. The perception by many providers that all health plans are part of an "evil empire" is one such example. While some health plans may have conducted their business in an enemy-like fashion by attempting to conquer providers, many other health plans have chosen other ways of doing business. In many cases, an enemy image begins to escalate conflict before the parties even reach the negotiating table. Expecting to confront an enemy, an unskilled negotiator will plan strategies and techniques in a manner similar to preparing to do battle. At the table, the slightest act of provocation can then disrupt an otherwise cooperative effort. Also, prejudicial images may cause actions and intentions to be misconstrued.

Over Simplification

Complex problems cannot be solved with simple solutions. The healthcare industry is extremely complex, and every action or agreement will cause multiple reactions. When a negotiator tries to over-simplify situations or prescribe simple solutions, objections will arise and conflict will escalate. When a physician is approached regarding a change in practice patterns to improve his utilization, the physician may answer, "But my patients are sicker than those of my colleagues." While this may or may not be true, conflict will increase by the challenging of the physician's performance without considering the details or complexity that may exist in measuring his utilization patterns. The simple concept of managed competition proposed by the Clinton administration encountered significant conflict from many industry sectors. The phrase, "The devil is in the details" was probably appropriate in that case and could have been one of the reasons for the ultimate failure of the reform initiative.

Conflict De-escalators

Just as some actions can escalate conflict, a negotiator can also de-escalate conflict. When conflict arises at the negotiating table, the skillful negotiator will manage the situation to reduce the conflict level. Every negotiator should understand and make use of conflict de-escalators. Conflict de-escalators can include understanding the price of failure, humanizing the other side, and face saving.

Understanding the Price of Failure

A skilled negotiator will attempt to explain to the opponent the consequences or price of failing to reach an agreement. The existence of the negotiation itself suggests that both parties would benefit by reaching an agreement. A negotiator could point out to the opponent that his or her BATNA is a price of failure and hopefully resume a more reasonable attitude. If a provider is being unreasonable in negotiating with a health plan the provider considers the enemy, the opponent may simply point out that the plan constitutes over 25 percent of the provider's revenue stream and that while the loss of the provider from its network was not a desirable outcome, a sufficient network of other providers from which to chose exists.

Humanizing the Other Side

Conflict resolution experts use the technique of humanizing the other party as a means to resolve or lessen conflict. Using this approach, negotiators attempt to get one party to understand the problem or issue from the other party's perspective. The parties may engage in a role-playing exercise and assume the role of the opponent and argue the opponent's positions. Parties often gain a greater understanding of the other side and the validity of its arguments when this approach is used. Eventually, the parties can return to the bargaining table and resume discussions in a more conciliatory manner.

The results are interesting when a corporate executive from a health system or health plan is asked to "walk in the shoes" of a physician. For the most part, these executives have never worked outside of a corporate environment and have always enjoyed steady paychecks, employment benefits, and a sense of economic security. When faced with the physician's situation, the executives quickly recognize the different perspective, needs, and interests of a physician. The different challenges and concerns of being a small business person suddenly become both apparent and valid.

Face Saving

Emotional outbursts and abrasive comments are not unusual during negotiations. While many individuals would like to react in a similar manner, the skillful negotiator will pass on such an opportunity and seek to get the negotiation back to a more productive tone. In negotiations where the opponent makes exaggerated comments, misstatements of fact, or outright lies, the tendency to punish the opponent must be avoided. Rather, the negotiator should acknowledge that the opponent may have been mistaken and allow him or her another opportunity to state a different fact or produce another argument. If you challenge the opponent with your opinion that he or she is not telling the truth, the opponent may strongly deny the allegation and conflict will escalate. Making an apology is another effective face-saving approach. While it is sometimes difficult to offer an apology or acknowledge a mistake in our litigious society, failure to do so will usually prolong a conflict.

Personal Tendencies in Dealing with Conflict

Not all people deal with conflict in a similar manner. While some may anticipate conflict and use it productively, others try to avoid conflict at all costs or refer conflict resolution to a third party. A good negotiator will understand his or her own tendencies in dealing with conflict, as well as the opponent's, and make appropriate changes when necessary. The following personalities tend to emerge during conflict.

Conflict Commandos

Conflict commandos will often take conflict situations to a superior or the board of trustees. They will not seek to deal with conflict at the negotiating table, but rather use a third party as a means of determining an outcome. Attorneys are commonly conflict commandos and seek to resolve conflict in front of a judge or jury. The main concern with conflict commandos is that neither party in the conflict has much to say in the final solution.

Conflict Conquerors

The conflict conqueror will tend to force a solution by creating bargaining power through the use of threats, political pressure, deadlines, and other strategies to resolve the conflict according to his position. The resolutions are usually one-sided and fail to incorporate any interest or good ideas of the opponent. Furthermore, the opponent subjected to the conqueror will usually be looking for revenge by subverting the agreement or getting even at the next opportunity.

Conflict Avoiders

Some individuals avoid any conflict during a negotiation and simply acquiesce to the opponent's solution. In most cases, the conflict does not go away but merely surfaces at a later point in the negotiation or during the implementation of the agreement. Moreover, others from the conflict avoider's organization may have to be brought in to ultimately resolve the conflict.

Conflict Soldiers

Conflict soldiers understand that conflict will be present, prepare for it, and assume responsibility for resolving it in a productive and workable solution. These negotiators understand that conflict will not go away and are willing to tackle it at the bargaining table. A skillful negotiator must belong to this group.

In summary, conflict in negotiations will always exist. It can be anticipated, managed and, hopefully, leveraged in a way that results in a better agreement. Look at conflict as the indicator that something needs adjustment and use it as catalyst to move the opponent in a positive direction. Understand the sources of conflict and be on a constant lookout for conflict escalators that may arise at the negotiating table. Seek to de-escalate conflict whenever possible to maintain an optimized negotiating environment.

DEALING WITH NON-NEGOTIATORS

A time may come in every negotiator's career when the negotiator encounters an opponent who will not, or can not, engage in the negotiation process. Many of these opponents seem to have attended the "stubbornness school of negotiation." For a variety of reasons, these individuals are unwilling to adopt a conciliatory tone and work toward reaching an agreement. The skillful negotiator must understand why the opponent is taking this approach and what can be done to initiate a negotiation.

Lack of Understanding of the Negotiation Process

One potential reason for the opponent's lack of willingness to engage in negotiations may simply be a lack of understanding of the process itself. Some negotiators believe that being stubborn, sticking to one's own position, and eventually wearing down the opponent is a desirable negotiating trait. These negotiators may not understand that negotiation is a conciliatory process and that give and take on both sides is required.

During a negotiation seminar with a group of medical staff leaders, one of the physicians presented his views on the process. The physician told the group that during his medical training he was told that after making his diagnosis and treatment decisions he was to stick to those positions and never compromise. Concessions were a sign of weakness or indecision. He then said that he carried the same sort of attitude to the negotiating table. You can easily see that this physician, along with some of his colleagues, could be extremely stubborn when it is time to make concessions in a negotiation.

Members of the legal profession may also have problems with understanding the negotiation process. During their legal education, very few receive any formal negotiating training, but rather are acquainted with what is known as the adversarial process as mentioned in a previous chapter. In this process, the objective of the attorney is to bring a dispute in front of a third party and seek to win his case, or his position, *in its entirety*. In doing so, attorneys seldom try to seek a middle ground on an issue but rather will attempt to try to win every point of his client's position. One of the major problems encountered when an attorney is present in a negotiation is when he overlays this adversarial approach, with its methods and attitudes, when the parties are still attempting to negotiate.

What do you do when the opponent does not seem to understand the negotiation process? First, try education. Explain the process and its steps, draw a diagram of the parties' ranges of settlement, and indicate that both parties will need to concede to reach the overlap. Suggest that the opponent add a person to the negotiating team who *does* understand the process, or simply bypass the nonnegotiator and go to someone else in the organization or department who will negotiate. However, be sure to tell the opponent you intend to go to another person in the organization. The opponent's reaction to your "going behind his back" will upset the relationship and possibly subvert a potential agreement.

Lack of Understanding of the Subject Being Negotiated

A negotiator may be unable to adequately engage in negotiations because of lack of understanding of the subject being addressed. A party who does not clearly understand the key issues or their implications may be unwilling to concede simply for fear of the unknown. For example, when reimbursement in the form of capitation was first presented to physicians, they could understand that they would be getting X dollars per member per month up front, yet many were still hesitant to sign the agreements. The physicians admitted that while the money was attractive, they were unsure whether they could handle the care of the patients within the dollar amounts proposed. Because the physicians did not understanding the amount of additional risk, many simply refused to sign capitated contracts until after their colleagues had done so and demonstrated the viability of this form of reimbursement.

Limited Authority

Stubbornness at the negotiating table may also be the result of company policies, budgetary limits, or commitments made to secondary parties to the agreement. In one case, a medical equipment company's legal department had told the salespeople to never concede on issues of liquidated damages. At the negotiating table, these salespeople might appear stubborn when, in fact, they had no room to concede. Questioning the salesperson might reveal the barrier, thereby enabling a request that the opponent's attorneys be present at the next negotiating session to resolve the issue.

Using good questioning techniques, a skillful negotiator can often identify the reason a party is being particularly stubborn. If the stubbornness is for lack of knowledge of the process, then an educational effort might be considered. If the subject matter is confusing, acquainting the opponent with the subject might be beneficial. If, on the other hand, the negotiator discovers that the opponent is not able to concede because of limited authority or commitments made to others, the negotiator may simply delay the negotiations on those issues until people with higher levels of authority are present.

DEALING WITH A "TAKE IT OR LEAVE IT" POSITION

The statement "take it or leave it" *often* indicates that no concessions are forthcoming nor will the other side continue to engage in the process of negotiation. It can also be used by a negotiator in a position of superior bargaining strength as a means to reach closure to a negotiation, as in the case of a final offer. In this case it may be extremely effective in getting just what the negotiator desires. At other times, a negotiator's use of the phrase may indicate a lack of understanding of the process and a belief that stubbornness is a desirable trait at the bargaining table. In some cases, the take it or leave it position is simply a bluff and an attempt to get concessions from the opponent when, in fact, the negotiator is still willing to make concessions.

How does a negotiator deal with a take it or leave it position? A good negotiator is prepared. Has the opponent used this technique in the past? If these types of threats have been used effectively in the past, expect an attempt to use a similar technique again. Even if the opponent has not used a take it or leave it approach in the past, a good negotiator will anticipate and prepare for the situation during prenegotiation preparation.

A skilled negotiator might wish to develop the ability to leave it. By being able to walk away from the negotiation and achieve an acceptable alternative elsewhere, the negotiator is in a strong position and the walkout or deadlock may have greater negative consequences for the opponent than the negotiator. A negotiator may even inform the opponent regarding acceptable alternatives and of the negative consequences to the opponent by not reaching an agreement.

Negotiations will arise, however, where you cannot leave it. Here the opponent's use of a take it or leave it is most effective for the opponent. Hospital executives frequently face situations where physicians who admit large numbers of patients to the hospital present the hospital with a take it or leave it proposition. The physicians have vastly superior bargaining power, and the use of this technique places the executives in a very difficult position. The skillful negotiator recognizes, however, that while the hospital may be forced to "take it" on the major issue or issues being discussed, the negotiator may still seek concessions that are of lesser importance to the opponent. Similarly, in dealing with a large health plan, a provider may not be able to negotiate the reimbursement rates being proposed and should not waste bargaining power doing so. Rather, a better use of the limited bargaining power would be to seek concessions on lesser issues such as payment terms, claims submission processes, and medical management issues.

Lastly, even in a situation where you may not be able to "leave it," a negotiator may want to do exactly that, at least temporarily if the negotiator believes that the opponent is bluffing. If this is the case, the opponent will quickly recognize that the position taken is not being accepted and no agreement will be reached. By recognizing the consequences of not achieving an agreement, the opponent may retract this stance and express a more flexible position or a willingness to start negotiating.

DEALING WITH HARDBALL NEGOTIATORS

Hardball negotiators play by their own rules and use pressure tactics such as threats and intimidation to prevail. While there is certainly some truth that a squeaky wheel gets the grease, recognize that the rest of the wagon needs attention also. In a similar fashion, the hardball negotiator usually pushes toward one-sided agreements with a logical outcome as a secondary consideration.

Hardball negotiators often get their way, and studies have indicated that these types of negotiators will prevail 60 to 80 percent of the time. In our modern, polite society people will often put their own needs aside to avoid conflict. Moreover, the responses of those negotiators willing to face off with a hardball negotiator tend to be emotional and result in less than optimal negotiations. The techniques used in hardball situations are primarily threatening, intimidating, or psychological in nature.

Threats

The primary purpose of a negotiator's threat is to increase bargaining power. However, the degree of bargaining power of the opponent's threat depends on how much bargaining power you give it. If you believe the threat is significant, the threat has considerable bargaining power. If, on the other hand, you do not see it as significant, then it may have very little effect. Negotiators tend to respond to threats emotionally rather than logically. This response may be due in part to a natural self-defense mechanism that immediately responds to any threatening situation. However, by responding quickly and emotionally, the negotiator may give more bargaining power to a threat than it deserves. Four steps can be taken to respond more logically to a threat.

1. Anticipate the threat. Try to anticipate the opponent's threats. Commonly, the opponent may tell you what the threat is prior to the negotiation. Why would the opponent do this? If you do not know the threat exists, you will not give it any bargaining power. This may be one of the reasons that unions are quick to provide a strike notice or a salesperson lets you know of a coming price increase. When meeting with a physician, hospital executives should always anticipate a threat of, "If you cannot give me what I need, I guess I will have to take my patients to the medical center down the street." In a managed care negotiation, a negotiator can expect a health plan negotiator to state, "If we can't reach agreement on this rate, I guess we'll have to use your competitor to meet our network needs." During prenegotiation preparation, spend some time working through worst-case scenarios to uncover your vulnerability to threats.

2. Determine whether the threat is real. Determining whether the threat is real is important because otherwise you will be giving away bargaining power. Consider whether the opponent will even carry out the threat. Could the physicians really move their practice to another institution? Would their patients, other members of their medical group, or their contracts allow it? Will the health plan want to send all their members to your competitor? Investigation may be required but it is usually possible to determine whether the threat is real or not.

If you discover that a threat is not real, either totally ignore the threat, or "negatively link" the threat. By ignoring the threat you essentially give it no bargaining power and force the opponent to negotiate based on other, more logical, arguments. In "negatively linking" a threat, the negotiator lets the opponent know that there will be negative consequences for both parties if the threat is carried out. For example, a negotiator might let the physicians know that by going down the street, you will be forced to recruit to your medical staff other physicians in their specialty and introduce competition for the referrals they receive from your medical staff.

3. Quantify the impact of the threat. The next step in dealing with threats is to quantify the impact of the threat on both parties. Determine whether, for example, the threat is a $5,000 per month threat or a $500,000 per month threat. One threat would obviously have greater bargaining power than the other. The opponent may tell you how bad the threat will hurt you, but by quantifying the threat, you have your own estimation of its significance rather than relying on the opponent's. If you have not estimated this amount, you are in a difficult position to argue with the opponent's estimate, which in most cases is exaggerated.

Calculate the effects of carrying out the threat on the opponent. Usually, a threat will have negative implications for both parties. If the health plan were to send its members to a competitor, what is the impact in terms of lessened competition from providers for their business or from the loss of prestige with your facility by not being part of the network?

Once you have estimated the impact of the threat on both parties, you are ready to assess the bargaining power to give to the threat. The bargaining power to give to the threat is related to the "net." By subtracting the impact of the threat on the opponent from the impact it will have on you, the negotiator can get a sense of its importance and its bargaining power. If a threat will hurt you considerably but not hurt the opponent too much, the net is a large positive and the threat should be attributed significant bargaining power. If the impact on both parties will be approximately equal, the net is zero and therefore no bargaining power should be given to the threat. In some cases, the negative implications for the person making the threat is greater than the person being threatened, thus the net result is a negative number.

$$\begin{array}{r} \text{Impact on Your Organization} \\ (-) \text{ Impact on Your Opponent} \\ \hline = \text{Bargaining Power (Net)} \end{array}$$

4. Develop a contingency plan. A good negotiator will develop a contingency plan in case a threat is carried out. Without a plan, the negative impact for the negotiator may be considerably greater than anticipated. On the other hand, if the negotiator advises the opponent of the negotiator's sound contingency plan or alternative, the opponent's bargaining power will be decreased. For example, during a nursing strike, a negotiator might consider the use of agency nurses, nurse supervisors, or the deferment of elective procedures as possible measures to mitigate the impact of a threat.

Also, by proposing an alternative to the threat, a negotiator might be able to avoid a threat from being carried out. A physician group that threatens to establish its own outpatient surgical center in direct competition with a hospital might be willing to look at a joint venture. While this alternative might not be as desirable as simply having no competing venture, it would be a preferable middle ground to having the physicians carry out their threat.

When dealing with hardball negotiators, resist giving in to avoid confrontation and try to reorient the negotiation toward a logical approach. In the book *Getting to Yes,* the authors refer to this as "negotiating jujitsu." The aim of the negotiator is to absorb the hardballer's technique and then redirect the negotiation in a more productive direction. By acknowledging the threat or abusive language, the negotiator can inform the opponent that threats will yield little in terms of resolving the situation. You can then suggest a more logic-based approach for arriving at an agreement that will satisfy both parties' interests.

Remember that a hardball negotiator attempts to bargain based on his own rules rather than through a process aimed at achieving a logic-based agreement. By choosing to play by the hardball negotiator's rules, you will often be tempted to counter with your own threats or acts of intimidation. Anyone who has ever witnessed such a situation will see a destructive process that it is the antithesis of negotiating from a logical, and optimized, approach.

REFERENCE

Fisher, R., W. Ury, and B. Patton. 1991. *Getting to Yes: Negotiating Agreement Without Giving In.* New York: Penguin Books.

Becoming A
Masterful Negotiator

How does one become a masterful negotiator? While mastering the negotiation process is an achievable goal for any healthcare executive, becoming proficient at the bargaining table does not occur simply by reading a few books on the subject or being a thoughtful and considerate individual. Becoming a masterful negotiator involves understanding the subject, knowing your own personal strengths and weaknesses, and continually seeking to improve your outcomes by trial and error at the bargaining table.

What steps must you take or what characteristics do you need to realize the goal of becoming a masterful negotiator? Become adept with the process itself, that is, understand different negotiation approaches, strategies, and techniques, and understand difficult negotiating situations and ways to deal with them. Cultivate personal characteristics that will allow both you and your opponent an opportunity to have fruitful discussions resulting in optimized agreements. Finally, and most importantly, be able to integrate these various elements to maximize their effectiveness resulting in favorable agreements for both sides. Negotiation is not a "one size fits all" process. No single approach will work best in all situations and with all opponents. The challenge in mastering negotiation is to assess each situation and opponent individually, develop a sound, reasoned approach and strategy beforehand, and implement that game plan effectively at the bargaining table.

UNDERSTANDING THE NEGOTIATION PROCESS

Understanding the negotiation process from prenegotiation preparation through the formal negotiation prepares you to not only recognize your strengths and weaknesses, but to identify ways to improve your performance. Understanding the approaches that can be used in negotiation is also important as you consider what combination might be appropriate in any given situation, as well as how to deal with the approaches your opponents may use.

Achieving optimized negotiating sessions is the goal for the masterful negotiator. You need to understand what preconditions exist for each situation and correct any deficiencies you find. Keeping the negotiations on the "high road" will require constant surveillance for situations that might bring your negotiations down to an arm-wrestling or transactional level. Using the proper negotiation techniques for any given situation requires a clear understanding of what is available and what will be appropriate and effective. Techniques that might work when you are in a strong bargaining power position may be totally ineffective when you are not. Adjusting the techniques for different situations and opponents is a clear sign of a masterful negotiator. In addition to using this book to gain understanding and insight into the process of negotiation, you are encouraged to seek out additional information to further develop your abilities and understanding of the negotiation process.

CHARACTERISTICS OF THE MASTERFUL NEGOTIATOR

In addition to understanding the process of negotiation itself, masterful negotiators also need to cultivate certain character traits. After watching thousands of healthcare executives engage in both real life and simulated negotiations, I believe certain characteristics are clearly evident in masterful negotiators. In your desire to master the negotiation process, you must honestly assess your own character traits and be willing to change them if necessary. The common characteristics of masterful negotiators are:

1. Honesty and integrity—Demonstrating honesty and integrity is a fundamental requirement of any optimized negotiation. Once the opponent sees that you consistently demonstrate such qualities, the opponent will be more likely to trust you. That trust will allow the opponent to develop a stronger personal relationship with you and approach you with openness. Without a sense of trust, the opponent may withhold certain interests and desires, preventing the frank and constructive discussions required for any optimized negotiation.

2. Flexibility—Being flexible allows you to adapt to changing situations, new information, and the simple element of change itself. A negotiator needs to constantly adapt strategies and techniques based on the opponent, relative bargaining power, and desired outcomes. Flexibility also allows the negotiator to consider new ideas or alternatives as potential solutions rather than simply rejecting them because "that is not the way we do things here."

3. Listening skills—Good negotiators are good listeners and do not attempt to bombard the opponent with arguments as a means to reach agreement. Instead, negotiators listen to the opponent, consider issues from the opponent's perspective, and propose solutions that can address both parties' interests. Good negotiators listen patiently without interrupting and try to understand both the content and feeling of the messages they receive. As Stephen Covey has suggested, "Seek first to understand, then to be understood."

4. Balance courage and consideration—Having the courage and firmness to stand up for your interests or positions is only part

of being a masterful negotiator. A good negotiator will also consider the validity of the opponent's positions. By being firm but also willing to consider the other party's interests, a skilled negotiator is more likely to reach mutually beneficial agreements. If this balance is skewed to one side or the other, one-sided agreements will often result.

5. Big-picture thinking—A masterful negotiator uses a big-picture" approach to negotiations, which requires understanding the interrelationships between the parties and the causes and effects on the entire system as a result of the agreement. Also, a masterful negotiator will keep the overall deal in proper perspective and not lose sight of the overall objectives and interests or get lost negotiating over minor issues or concerns. Masterful negotiators do not ignore the details, but they do understand that agreement on minor issues is irrelevant if the major issues or interests are not addressed or go unmet.

6. Value orientation—A successful agreement adds value for *all* parties. If one party feels the agreement is not serving his interests, that party may look to subvert the agreement. Agreements that do not add value will seldom stand the test of time. The breakup of a number of healthcare systems formed in the last several years are examples of agreements where no value was ever created.

7. Ability to make concessions—Masterful negotiators almost always possess a mindset that allows them to share or give to others. Making concessions is not perceived as a loss of control or resources but rather a necessary step in achieving the objectives of the overall agreement. On the other hand, negotiators that possess a scarcity mentality are hesitant to make concessions, viewing them as a loss.

8. Fairness—Achieving a "fair" agreement for all parties is the objective in a negotiation. A masterful negotiator, even when in a position of superior bargaining power, will stop negotiating before the agreement begins to look unfair to the opponent. A fair agreement can be easily implemented.

9. Patience and timing—Diligent and thoughtful, a masterful negotiator seldom rushes into an agreement. Time spent in negotiating good agreements will be returned many times over during the implementation phase of a well-constructed agreement. A sense of timing regarding when to introduce issues, make concessions, and to close an agreement is a skill the masterful negotiator commonly possesses.

INTEGRATING PROCESS WITH PERSONALITY

Becoming a true master of the negotiation process requires the ability to integrate knowledge of the process with desirable personal characteristics. One without the other will seldom yield optimized agreements. Understanding and wanting to optimize the negotiation will be difficult, if not impossible, if the opponent does not trust you or does not believe you are willing to consider the opponent's interests or positions. Similarly, while you may be an honest individual who is willing to make concessions to come to an agreement, if you have no knowledge of the negotiation process you stand a chance of achieving a one-sided agreement in favor of the opponent.

The skilled negotiator is able to adapt approaches, techniques, and strategies based on a variety of factors. Negotiating styles, relative bargaining power, past strategies or techniques, deadliness, and conflict concerns must all factor into your strategy. What might work most effectively in a collective bargaining situation facing a "seasoned" negotiator from the union will almost certainly not be the same approach you would use when dealing with a valued member of your medical staff. Understanding your own negotiating style and what you are comfortable with can also help you find a proper approach.

One final idea in improving your abilities as a negotiator is to learn from your experiences. Think over your past negotiations and consider what worked, what did not work, and what you might do differently. There has probably never been a "perfect" negotiation where you would not change one thing. Therefore, by looking at your negotiating successes and failures, you will certainly find things that you might reconsider next time you approach the bargaining table. Some negotiators keep a journal for making notations about each negotiation, jotting down areas for improvements and ideas that were extremely effective. By reflecting on your past experience, you will begin to see where your strengths and weaknesses are, allowing you to change your negotiation styles, approaches, strategies, and techniques.

With these ideas in mind, your journey to becoming a masterful negotiator is well underway. Mastering the negotiation process is an essential skill for today's healthcare executive and can yield the agreements that will be necessary for your organization to thrive in this exciting industry.

About the Author

CHRIS LAUBACH IS the president of the Center for Management Programs in Agoura Hills, California. For more than 20 years, the company has conducted more than 500 negotiation training seminars for healthcare executives. Mr. Laubach has personally trained more than 7,500 healthcare professionals in the general process of negotiation, managed care negotiations, organized labor negotiations, and conflict resolution. His clients have included hospital executives, physician executives, managed care organizations, and major suppliers to the healthcare industry.

Over the past two decades, Mr. Laubach has researched, developed, and instructed numerous seminars on a variety of healthcare topics including managed care, physician practice acquisition, quality improvement, negotiating skills, and hospital finance. He is active in conducting educational retreats for trustees, medical staff members, senior and middle-management personnel, and managed care organizations.

He is a lead faculty member of the American College of Healthcare Executives and conducts numerous seminars for the College. He is the lead faculty in teaching ACHE programs on the "Process and

Techniques of Negotiating," "Advanced Negotiating," and "Managing Healthcare Facility Design and Construction Programs."

Prior to his involvement in the healthcare industry, Mr. Laubach was the vice president of Project Development and Licensing for SGI International, an energy technology company in La Jolla, California. He was responsible for worldwide licensing and project development negotiations with major coal companies in the United Sates, Australia, and Eastern Europe.

Mr. Laubach graduated with a bachelor of science degree in construction management from California State University at San Luis Obispo and master's in business administration degree from the University of California.